Anger
MANAGEMENT

**HOW TO TAKE CONTROL
OF YOUR EMOTIONS
AND FIND JOY
IN LIFE**

JUDY DYER

Anger Management:
How to Take Control of Your Emotions
and Find Joy in Life
by Judy Dyer

© Copyright 2020 by Judy Dyer

All Rights Reserved.

No part of this publication may be reproduced, distributed, or transmitted in any form or by any means, including photocopying, recording, or other electronic or mechanical methods, without the prior written permission of the publisher, except in the case of brief quotations embodied in reviews and certain other noncommercial uses permitted by copyright law.

Disclaimer: This book is designed to provide accurate and authoritative information in regard to the subject matter covered. By its sale, neither the publisher nor the author is engaged in rendering psychological or other professional services. If expert assistance or counseling is needed, the services of a competent professional should be sought.

ISBN: 979-8620852451

ALSO BY JUDY DYER

Empath: A Complete Guide for Developing Your Gift and Finding Your Sense of Self

The Empowered Empath: A Simple Guide on Setting Boundaries, Controlling Your Emotions, and Making Life Easier

The Highly Sensitive: How to Stop Emotional Overload, Relieve Anxiety, and Eliminate Negative Energy

Narcissist: A Complete Guide for Dealing with Narcissism and Creating the Life You Want

Empaths and Narcissists: 2 Books in 1

Empath and The Highly Sensitive: 2 Books in 1

Borderline Personality Disorder: A Complete BPD Guide for Managing Your Emotions and Improving Your Relationships

CONTENTS

Introduction		7
Your Free Gift – Heyoka Empath		13
Chapter 1:	Do You Have an Anger Problem?	19
Chapter 2:	Why are Some People More Likely to Get Angry?	32
Chapter 3:	Breaking the Anger Cycle	39
Chapter 4:	Understanding & Handling Anger in Relationships	51
Chapter 5:	How to Grow Your Emotional Intelligence	66
Chapter 6:	Mindfulness for Anger Management	79
Chapter 7:	Forgiving Others & Letting Go of Grudges	88
Chapter 8:	Anger Management for Parents	99
Chapter 9:	Anger & Jealousy	111
Chapter 10:	Handling Anger At Work	124
Chapter 11:	How To Handle Difficult People	138
Chapter 12:	Lifestyle Changes & Anger Management	149
Conclusion		161

INTRODUCTION

Do you ever feel so mad you might explode? Would you describe yourself as "fiery," "hot-tempered," or "difficult to live with"? Maybe you take pride in your no-nonsense approach to life—or maybe you've realized it's time to change. If you've picked up this book, you already know that your anger has become a major problem.

Pathological anger can ruin your relationships, career, and health if you don't take action. The good news is that you can and will learn to control it if you follow the techniques in this guide.

You aren't alone in your struggle. Eight percent of the adult population finds it hard to control their temper. Anyone can develop an anger problem.[1] Anger may be a stereotypically male issue, but lots of women also need help controlling their rage.

In this book, we'll dive deep into the topic of anger. You'll discover:

- Whether your anger is normal or pathological
- How anger affects your body, relationships, and mental health
- Why you get angry, and why it's so difficult to calm down

- Proven, easy-to-use techniques that will ease your anger
- How to manage stress and lead a healthier lifestyle
- How to improve your relationships and reduce conflict
- How to use mindfulness to release anger and old grudges

It's never too late to change your attitude, conquer your self-defeating beliefs, and learn new skills. Taking charge of your emotions and keeping your anger under control is key if you want to develop your emotional intelligence (EQ).[2] It doesn't matter how angry you are—there is always hope. If you persevere, things will start to change quickly.

Turn the page to get started.

JOIN OUR FACEBOOK GROUP

In order to maximize the value you receive from this book, I highly encourage you to join our tight-knit community on Facebook. Here we focus on mastering your gifts as an Empath, but you will be able to connect and share with other like-minded readers to continue your growth.

Taking this journey alone is not recommended, and this can be an excellent support network for you.

It would be great to connect with you there,

Judy Dyer

To Join, Visit: www.pristinepublish.com/empathgroup

DOWNLOAD THE AUDIO VERSION OF THIS BOOK FREE

If you love listening to audiobooks on-the-go or would enjoy a narration as you read along, I have great news for you. You can download the audiobook version of *Anger Management* for FREE (Regularly $14.95) just by signing up for a FREE 30-day Audible trial!

Visit: www.pristinepublish.com/audiobooks

YOUR FREE GIFT - HEYOKA EMPATH

A lot of empaths feel trapped, as if they've hit a glass ceiling they can't penetrate. They know there's another level to their gift, but they can't seem to figure out what it is. They've read dozens of books, been to counselling, and confided in other experienced empaths, but that glass ceiling remains. They feel alone, and alienated from the rest of the world because they know they've got so much more to give, but can't access it. Does this sound like you?

The inability to connect to your true and authentic self is a tragedy. Being robbed of the joy of embracing the full extent of your humanity is a terrible misfortune. The driving force of human nature is to live according to one's own sense of self, values, and emotions. Since the beginning of time, philosophers, writers, and scholars have argued that authenticity is one of the most important elements of an individual's well-being.

When there's a disconnect between a person's inner being and their expressions, it can be psychologically damaging. Heyokas are the most powerful type of empaths, and many of them are not fully aware of who they are. While other empaths experience feelings of overwhelm and exhaustion from absorbing others' energy and emotions, heyoka empaths experience an additional aspect of exhaustion in that they are fighting a constant battle with their inability to be completely authentic.

The good news is that the only thing stopping you from becoming your authentic self is a lack of knowledge. You need to know exactly who you are so you can tap into the resources that have been lying dormant within you. In this bonus e-book, you'll gain in-depth information about the seven signs that you're a heyoka empath, and why certain related abilities are such powerful traits. You'll find many of the answers to the questions you've been searching for your entire life such as:

- Why you feel uncomfortable when you're around certain people
- How you always seem to find yourself on the right path even though your decisions are not based on logic or rationale
- The reason you get so offended when you find out others have lied to you
- Why you analyze everything in such detail
- The reason why humor is such an important part of your life
- Why you refuse to follow the crowd, regardless of the consequences
- The reason why strangers and animals are drawn to you

There are three main components to authenticity: understanding who you are, expressing who you are, and letting the world experience who you are. Your first step on this journey is to know who you are, and with these seven signs that you're a heyoka empath, you'll find out. I've included snippets about the first three signs in this description to give you full confidence that you're on the right track:

Sign 1: You Feel and Understand Energy

Heyoka empaths possess a natural ability to tap into energy. They can walk into a room and immediately discern the atmosphere. When an individual walks past them, they can literally see into their soul because they can sense the aura that person is carrying. But empaths also understand their own energy, and they allow it to guide them. You will often hear this ability referred to as "the sixth sense." The general consensus is that only a few people have this gift. But the reality is that everyone was born with the ability to feel energy; it's just been demonized and turned into something spooky, when in actual fact, it's the most natural state to operate in.

Sign 2: You are Led by Your Intuition

Do you find that you just know things? You don't spend hours, days, and weeks agonizing over decisions, you can just feel that something is the right thing to do, and you go ahead and do it. That's because you're led by your intuition and you're connected to the deepest part of yourself. You know your soul, you listen to it, and you trust it. People like Oprah Winfrey, Steve Jobs and Richard Branson followed their intuition steadfastly and it led them to become some of the most successful people in the history of the world.

Living from within is the way we were created to be, and those who trust this ability will find their footing in life a lot more quickly than others. Think of it as a GPS system: when it's been programmed properly, it will always take you to your destination via the fastest route.

Sign 3: You Believe in Complete Honesty

In general, empaths don't like being around negative energy, and there's nothing that can shift a positive frequency faster than dishonesty. Anything that isn't the truth is a lie, even the tiny ones that we excuse away as "white lies." And as soon as they're released from someone's mouth, so is negative energy. Living an authentic life requires complete honesty at all times, and although the truth may hurt, it's better than not being able to trust someone. Heyoka empaths get very uncomfortable in the presence of liars. They are fully aware that the vibrations of the person don't match the words they are saying. Have you ever experienced a brain freeze mid-conversation? All of a sudden you just couldn't think straight, you couldn't articulate yourself properly, and things just got really awkward? That's because your empath antenna picked up on a lie.

Heyoka Empath: 7 Signs You're A Heyoka Empath & Why It's So Powerful is a revolutionary tool that will help you transition from uncertainty to complete confidence in who you are. In this easy-to-read guide, I will walk you through exactly what makes you a heyoka empath. I've done the research for you, so no more spending hours, days, weeks, and even years searching for answers, because everything you need is right here in this book.

You have a deep need to share yourself with the world, but you've been too afraid because you knew something was missing. The information within the pages of this book is the missing piece in the jigsaw puzzle of your life. There's no turning back now!

Get *Heyoka Empath* for Free by Visiting

www.pristinepublish.com/empathbonus

CHAPTER 1:

DO YOU HAVE AN ANGER PROBLEM?

Perhaps you get angry when you feel disrespected, or maybe you fly into a rage when you see someone else being mistreated. Anger is a normal part of the human experience. Unfortunately, some of us are easily consumed by anger. If left unchecked, anger can become a habit. In this chapter, we're going to look at what anger is, how it shows up in everyday life, and how to tell the difference between normal and pathological anger.

WHAT DOES ANGER FEEL LIKE?

Let's look at an example:

> *James drops in at the corner store to pick up a granola bar for breakfast on his way to work. He's hungry, tired, and worried about a presentation he has to give that day. There's a long queue at the checkout. James senses his stress levels rising and feels mildly irritated. He thinks to himself, "Why is this store so busy?" Suddenly, two teenagers push in front of him. He has to fight hard*

to hold back the urge to swear. He grits his teeth and feels his stomach clench. For the next hour, James feels grumpy and irritable. Every little thing at work annoys him, and he is short-tempered with his personal assistant. His team mutters, "The boss is in one of his bad moods again."

As we can see in James' story, anger is more than a feeling. It's more helpful to think of it as a mind-body experience, complete with both angry thoughts and physical symptoms.

Exercise: When Did You Last Get Angry?

When was the last time you felt really mad? Close your eyes, replay the memory, and tune into your body. Can you identify what exactly made you so angry? What were you thinking and feeling at the time? What happened in your body?

YOUR BODY & ANGER

It takes only a couple of seconds for our bodies to release the hormones that trigger the physical symptoms of anger. When you get mad, adrenalin, cortisol, and noradrenaline raise your blood pressure and heart rate.

When you get angry, you might:

- Feel very hot
- Start to sweat
- Suddenly need to go to the toilet
- Feel your chest tighten

- Feel your stomach tighten or churn
- Have heart palpitations
- Struggle to think clearly

Anger and adrenalin are energizing. They help your body prepare to fight back against the thing or person who is threatening to harm you.[3]

Common Anger Triggers[4]

- Verbal or physical assault
- A physical or psychological threat to you or someone you care about
- Someone acting in a way you think is immoral or distasteful
- Being prevented from reaching an important goal
- Being insulted
- Being excluded
- Unfair treatment, especially if you can't fight back
- Having your possessions damaged or destroyed
- Receiving disappointing news
- Being lied to

Is Anger Always Bad?

Some anger can be a positive force. Anger motivates us to stand up for ourselves if we are threatened. Healthy anger spurs us to work for the greater good; societal change is often triggered by moral outrage. Feeling and releasing anger can be a normal coping mechanism in stressful situations.

If we were all laid back and indifferent to the injustices of the world, the human race wouldn't have lasted very long.

This book isn't about healthy anger, which is constructive, infrequent, and proportionate to the situation. It's about identifying abnormal anger patterns and tackling them before they get out of control. When you overreact to a person or situation that doesn't present any real danger or threat, this is known as "pathological anger." Pathological anger can be highly destructive. If you are prone to anger, it's your responsibility to make changes.

Common Myths about Anger

Anger can be hard to talk about, often because we feel ashamed of it. There are many myths surrounding anger. In this section, we'll sort fact from fiction.

Exercise: How Much Do You Really Know About Anger?

As you read through the next section, make a mark every time you come across a myth you thought was true. Have you learned anything new? If you believed some of the myths, where did you learn them?

Here are some of the most common:

Myth: If I get angry, I'm a bad person.

Truth: Having feelings never makes you a bad person. Emotions are normal. It's what you do when you feel angry that counts.

Myth: If you have angry or abusive parents, you are destined to become an angry person.

Truth: It's true that growing up in an abusive home can make some people more vulnerable to developing anger problems. But this doesn't apply to everyone. What's more, some people become very timid because they are afraid of repeating their parents' behaviors. We'll explore this issue in more depth later.

Myth: Only men get angry.

Truth: Both men and women experience anger. Research shows that men and women express their anger in different ways. Men are more likely to become physically aggressive, whereas women tend to use indirect tactics, such as shunning the person who made them angry.[5]

Myth: Anger is a personality trait or habit that can't be cured.

Truth: Fortunately, this is not the case. Angry people can learn new, better ways to manage their rage.

Myth: Anger is a problem for young people. They usually grow out of it.

Truth: While it's true that teenagers and young people are prone to mood swings, they rarely "grow out of" a serious anger problem. Anger management is useful for people of all ages.

Myth: All anger feels the same.

Truth: Anger can take many different forms. Some people overreact and explode in the face of short-term threats but forget them quickly. Others are relatively good at dealing with minor irritations, but nurse grudges for years.

Myth: Taking drugs or drinking alcohol makes some people angry.

Truth: Mind-altering substances can lower your inhibitions. This makes it more likely that you will express thoughts and emotions you would normally keep under wraps. At the same time, no substance can "make" someone angry. Drinking or taking drugs does not fundamentally alter your personality.

Myth: If you can learn to ignore your anger, it will just go away.

Truth: If you try to suppress angry feelings, they will usually show up later in the form of unhealthy coping mechanisms, arguments, or aggression.

Myth: It's best to blow off steam when you feel angry because it will make you feel better.

Truth: If you get into the habit of "blowing up" whenever you get mad, you will train yourself to explode whenever you feel angry. This is not a reliable coping strategy. Research shows that venting about anger can make you feel worse.[6]

Anger shouldn't be ignored, but neither should you give yourself permission to vent whenever you feel like it. The best way to manage your anger is to understand where it comes from, work with others to resolve conflicts, and learn how to express it in a safe, constructive way.

Myth: Unless you get angry, other people will take advantage of you.

Truth: Assertive communication, rather than anger, is the best way of standing up for yourself. Assertive people look out for their own interests, but they also respect other people. By contrast, angry people assume that their rights take precedence over everyone else.

Myth: Anger is easy to spot.

Truth: Some people make it very clear when they are angry, but others hide their emotions. Others take their feelings out on themselves rather than lashing out at those who hurt them. They might self-harm, isolate themselves, or tell themselves that they don't deserve even the essentials of life, such as food or sleep.

ANGER & MENTAL HEALTH PROBLEMS

Anger and mental health is a complicated topic. If you have been diagnosed with a mental illness, it's a good idea to learn how mental health and anger are linked. In some cases, anger can be a symptom of mental illness. For example, if you experience paranoid delusions, you might feel very angry and suspicious. If you have a personality disorder, such as Borderline Personality Disorder (BPD), your view of yourself and the world might make you more likely to experience destructive mood swings.

According to the mental health charity Mind, anger can also worsen the symptoms of mental illness, resulting in a downward spiral.[7] For example, if you are ashamed of your inability to control your temper, your self-esteem might suffer. You may start having thoughts like, "Why can't I just be normal?" Over time, this type of thinking can leave you feeling depressed and misunderstood.

Anger can also be linked to substance abuse and addiction. In the last chapter of this book, which addresses lifestyle changes and anger, you'll learn more about the link between alcohol, drugs, and anger.

If you are receiving treatment for a mental illness, you can use the ideas in this book in conjunction with medication or psychotherapy, but check with your doctor or therapist first. Most forms of therapy are compatible with the approach in this book, but your mental health professional may want you to tackle the exercises in a specific order; always follow their advice. They will probably be delighted that you are taking time to educate yourself about anger because proactive clients are more likely to recover.

Violent Thoughts

Some people regularly have intrusive, upsetting thoughts about harming or killing other people or animals. If you have this problem, you might assume it means you are an angry or dangerous person. In fact, it's more likely to be a sign of anxiety or obsessive-compulsive disorder (OCD).

Having these thoughts, no matter how vivid or compelling they may seem, doesn't mean you will ever act on them. However, they can cause a lot of distress. Make an appointment to see your doctor as soon as possible if intrusive thoughts are making you upset or depressed.[8] Health professionals know that these thoughts are actually quite common, even though most people don't talk about them. They should reassure you and refer you to a therapist or counselor for help. Medication can reduce the number of upsetting thoughts you have and make them less intense.

Is Your Anger Normal?

How do you tell when your anger has crossed the line? Let's look at key indicators that suggest a serious anger problem.[9]

1. **Your anger feels too strong to handle**
   Does your mind go blank when you get mad? Does it feel as though you are completely out of control? If so, it's time to practice strategies to get your feelings in check.

2. **You get angry on a regular basis**
   Occasional anger is normal, but flying into a rage several times per week or day is not. If you can't remember the last time you felt relaxed and contented, that's a big red flag. Angry people tend to dwell on people and events that have made them angry, which in turn makes them more likely to overreact in the future.

3. **You get angry over things that don't bother other people**

   We all have our pet peeves and hot-button issues, but if you blow up at minor things that don't faze anyone else, you need to learn new ways to cope with your feelings.

4. **Your anger is affecting your relationships**

   Anger is not endearing. If you don't address your anger, don't be surprised if your friends and relatives choose to spend less time with you. Angry people can be scary. If you have children, your anger can make you a less effective and stressed-out parent. Children who grow up with an angry mother or father can develop problems of their own as teens and adults.

5. **Your anger is affecting your work**

   Dwelling on angry thoughts impairs your concentration, which can have a cumulative effect on your work performance. Anger also makes forming positive relationships with your co-workers difficult. If you lash out at your fellow employees, customers, or your boss, you might lose your job. At the very least, you will earn a reputation as someone who is difficult to work with. This will harm your long-term career prospects.

6. **Your anger leads to aggression or violence**

   It is neither normal nor healthy to lash out at others, and it is absolutely unacceptable to assault someone in a fit of rage. If your behavior has landed you in trouble with the law, it's essential you make changes as soon as possible.

7. You use unhealthy coping mechanisms to deal with your anger

In a bid to control their anger, some people try using alcohol, drugs, or addictive behaviors to distract themselves or calm down. This might work in the short term, but causes more problems over time. For instance, if you get into the habit of drinking every time you want to suppress your anger, you could eventually become dependent on alcohol.

You don't have to be angry every day to have an anger problem. Even if you only have an angry episode every couple of weeks, that can still be enough to have a major impact on your life.

Exercise: Keeping an Anger Record

Over the next week, keep an anger log. All you need is a notebook or notetaking app on your phone. Whenever you experience a fit of anger, make a note of it. Write down the date, time, who you were with, and what happened. For every episode, give it an intensity rating on a scale of 1-10, where 10 means you could not have felt angrier. This exercise will give you insight into how your anger affects your life, and it will give you a boost of motivation to make changes. If you can, keep filling in your anger log for a month. The more data you have, the better.

Anger & Your Physical Health

Getting angry on a regular basis harms your physical health. For example, chronic anger increases your risk of stroke. According to the American Academy of Neurology, people who have had a stroke often report feeling intense negative emotions, including anger, in the two hours prior to the onset of their symptoms.[10]

When you feel stressed or angry, the muscles at the back of your scalp and neck tighten. This can cause benign but very painful headaches. Breathing slowly and deeply, in through your nose and out through your mouth, can relieve the pain, but it's better to manage the negative emotions that made you tense in the first place.

Anger can also harm your heart. Short bursts of anger aren't a problem, but a general tendency towards anger puts you at greater risk of coronary heart disease (CHD). In a study of 12,986 people, researchers found that people with high scores on measures of trait anger were twice as likely to develop CHD than those with low levels of anger.[11]

Finally, a 2015 study found a link between trait anger and Type 2 diabetes. Participants who displayed high levels of anger were 50% more likely to be diagnosed with the disease over an 11-year period. Angrier participants consumed more calories and exercised less often, which in turn increased their risk. Research into anger and chronic diseases is still ongoing, but we already have enough evidence to say with confidence that taking control of your anger will benefit your health.

RECOGNITION IS THE FIRST STEP TO CHANGE

If you've realized you have a problem with anger, take a moment to congratulate yourself. Most angry people never change because they are unwilling to take responsibility for their behaviors.

You may be wondering why you find it hard to keep your temper when others around you stay calm. In the next chapter, we'll look at why some people are more likely than others to develop pathological anger.

SUMMARY

- Anger isn't always destructive. We all get angry sometimes, and it can serve a healthy purpose.
- Anger is comprised of feelings and physical sensations.
- Anger triggers differ from person to person, but common triggers include deception, injustice, and being blocked from achieving a goal.
- It's important to separate fact from fiction when talking about anger.
- Anger becomes problematic if it interferes with your day-to-day life and damages your relationships.
- Anger poses risks to your physical health, and mental health and anger are closely linked for some people.

CHAPTER 2:

WHY ARE SOME PEOPLE MORE LIKELY TO GET ANGRY?

In this chapter, you'll learn about the biological and social causes of pathological anger. This book is focused on practical strategies you can use to control your temper. However, because lots of people are curious about where anger comes from, this section outlines a few interesting studies and theories.

Is Anger Genetic?

Studies of identical and non-identical twins suggest that about 50% of the variance in aggressive behavior is due to genetic differences.[1,2] So, if two random people from the population were to be tested using an anger measurement scale, differences in their genetic profiles would account for half the difference between their scores.

This doesn't mean you are destined to be an angry person for the rest of your life just because your family happens to be hot-tempered. No therapist or doctor would ever tell you to stop trying to control your anger on the basis that your parents had a similar problem. You may need to accept that controlling your anger will be harder for you than it is for others, but that doesn't mean you can't improve.

FAMILY BACKGROUND

If you've experienced adverse childhood events (ACE), such as abuse or the early death of a parent, you are more likely to have difficulty regulating your emotions. Research suggests you are also more likely to develop mental health problems, such as depression and personality disorders.[13] As you know, mental illness can worsen anger problems, and anger can worsen symptoms of a mental illness.

If you've spent any time caring for children, you'll know that they quickly pick up on adults' behaviors. Psychologists have known for a long time that we learn by watching others. If a child grows up in a home with people who can't (or won't) regulate their feelings, they may learn that expressing anger whenever you feel like it is normal and acceptable. This does not mean that every child who grew up in an unstable home develops an anger problem as an adult, but upbringing does often play a part in how we relate to other people.

Exercise: Anger in Your Family

Did you grow up in an angry home? What kind of impression did these experiences leave on you? Make a list. First, write down everyone who spent a lot of time in your home when you were a child—your mother, siblings, father, aunts, uncles, and so on.

Next, assign them an anger score. On a scale of 1-10, how angry were they? Finally, write down what you think they taught you about anger. Consider whether these experiences still influence you today.

Here's how a child's family background shapes their experience of anger:[14]

Observational learning: Children imitate what their parents do, especially if it gets results. For example, if a child sees that their mother gets her own way when she shouts and screams, the child learns that being angry is a good tool for manipulating other people and getting what you want.

Parenting practices: Parents who are willing and able to talk about emotions raise children who grow up emotionally balanced. Parents who deny their own emotions—or those of their own children—create a home environment where no one feels safe to express themself.

Children who don't get the chance to practice exploring and handling their own feelings grow up not knowing how to handle their anger. Children who are punished for showing their emotions don't shut down; they just find other, less healthy ways of expressing them.

STRESS & ANGER

Almost everyone feels more irritable when they're under stress. It's hard to stay calm and peaceful when problems are mounting up and the pressure is on. If you've been making some big changes to your life recently, such as moving or starting a new job, you might be more vulnerable than usual to feelings of anger.

Exercise: What's Been Going on in Your Life Recently?

Has your life changed in any major way over the past year? It can take months to settle into a new routine or adapt to a new lifestyle. A single event can trigger lots of smaller problems or sources of stress. For example, having a baby is a wonderful life event, but transitioning to parenthood also means you will deal with sleepless nights, more mess around the house, and possibly more arguments with your partner. If you make a list of all your major and minor sources of stress, you might be surprised by how much you are trying to deal with!

You might assume that your anger will pass when your circumstances settle down, and in some cases, you'd be right. Unfortunately, some people get into the habit of being angry and get stuck a pattern of overreacting to minor problems.

Anger and stress can feed into one another. For example, if your anger problems get you into trouble at work, you might feel stressed because you worry about being fired. The stress can then make you even more prone to angry outbursts.[15]

WHEN PHYSICAL HEALTH CONDITIONS CAUSE ANGER

Anyone who begins to feel angrier for no particular reason should see their doctor. This is because some physical illnesses can cause mood swings and rage.

If you see a doctor about your anger, they might run tests to check for the following:

1. **Hormonal conditions and imbalances**
   If you are female and feel particularly angry in the week or two leading up to your period, you may be suffering from premenstrual dysphoric disorder (PMDD). It's normal to feel more irritable than usual at this point in your cycle, but a minority of women experience extreme rage and mood swings that interfere with their lives. Keeping a mood diary will help your doctor make a diagnosis. The doctor may also give you a physical examination and blood tests to rule out other conditions.[16]

   Hormone imbalances can also affect men. If you are male and between the ages of 40 and 60, there's a small chance that your anger and irritability is caused by a combination of low testosterone and elevated cortisol. Along with mood changes, these imbalances also cause physical symptoms, such as hot flashes and night sweats. Your doctor can diagnose the problem with a blood test and by asking you about your medical history. Testosterone replacement therapy can ease your symptoms.[17]

2. **Blood sugar problems and diabetes**
   Blood sugar fluctuations can cause mood swings. If your blood sugar suddenly drops, you might feel hungry, irritable, and have trouble concentrating. Symptoms usually go away when you eat some-

thing sugary. Talk to your doctor if you suspect this happens to you.[18]

If you have already been diagnosed with diabetes but are having problems controlling your blood sugar, ask your doctor whether your condition could be having an effect on your mood. In some cases, high sugars also can cause mood problems.

3. **Neurological problems**

Organic diseases of the brain and nervous system can also cause anger and mood swings.[19] Parkinson's disease, epilepsy, and tumors are just three examples. Head injuries can also trigger changes in personality and mood.

It's important to note that none of these factors are excuses. If your anger makes someone else feel scared, they won't feel better knowing that your genetic makeup, family background, or something else is to blame. We all have a responsibility to handle our own emotions, for our own sake and that of other people around us.

FAULTY THINKING PATTERNS & COPING MECHANISMS

Genetics, upbringing, stress, and health conditions can all make anger problems more likely. However, they don't actually explain what happens the moment you feel angry. Understanding the factors that predispose you to anger is empowering, but that knowledge doesn't help you take back control when the red mist descends.

To make real progress, you need to learn about the links between your core beliefs, triggers, behaviors, and coping mechanisms. You need to understand why anger tends to follow a predictable pattern and how it leads to ongoing conflict in relationships. Angry people tend to hold unhelpful beliefs about the world and other people, and they often have problems dealing with strong emotions of any kind. Over the coming chapters, we'll look at these topics in greater depth.

Summary

- There are several factors that influence susceptibility to anger problems, including genetics and family relationships.
- Most people are more liable to become angry when they're under stress.
- It's a good idea to rule out physical causes if your anger problems started suddenly.
- Learning about factors that make you vulnerable to anger is empowering, but it's just the beginning of your journey in developing better coping skills.

CHAPTER 3:

BREAKING THE ANGER CYCLE

Now that you know what anger is and the factors that make someone more predisposed to anger problems, you're ready to learn more about the anger response. In this chapter, you'll learn how events, thoughts, feelings, and behaviors interact to create and maintain the anger cycle.

THE ANGER CYCLE

Here's how an anger response typically unfolds:

1. **Triggering event: Something happens to annoy you.**

    This might be another person's actions, a situation beyond your control, or even a recollection of something that made you angry in the past. For example, dealing with a difficult customer at work, losing your keys, or remembering a time your friend insulted you, are all potential triggers.

2. **Negative thoughts: Irrational thoughts and conclusions start to pop up.**

    For example, if you have to deal with a difficult

customer, you might think, "I hate handling customers" or "I'm awful at my job. I shouldn't get so angry with other people."

3. **Emotional response: Your negative thoughts trigger unpleasant emotions.**

   To continue with the above example, you might feel shame if you think you are "awful" at your job.

4. **Physical symptoms kick in: Because your body and mind are closely linked, you start experiencing symptoms triggered by adrenalin and cortisol.**

   You may shake, sweat, feel flushed, need to go to the bathroom, or feel sick. Your body language starts to show the telltale signs of anger. For example, you may clench your fists.

5. **Behavioral response: You act on your thoughts and emotions, perhaps by arguing, yelling, crying, withdrawing or criticizing others.**

   Your behaviors can trigger another chain of events that make you spiral out of control. For example, suppose you get into an argument with your co-worker that ends with you shouting at them. Your co-worker reports you to your boss, which makes you angry all over again. Destructive people may go through this cycle several times in one day, which can be exhausting.

Putting It All Together: An Example

Maria has taken her two young sons, Robbie and Alex, to visit her sister and brother-in-law. It's a hot day, and the family is sitting out in the yard. The boys are playing in the sandbox. Robbie and Alex bicker for a couple of minutes before Robbie suddenly hits Alex with his spade. This triggers Maria's anger. She thinks, "Why can't they just behave themselves for ten minutes? I must be a bad mother to have such naughty children!" Feeling flustered and embarrassed by their behavior, she rushes to the sandbox and starts shouting at her sons. Robbie and Alex feel scared and start to cry, which makes the situation even more upsetting for everyone.

All parents get exasperated from time to time. Maria isn't the first parent to shout, and she won't be the last. However, if she often overreacts and becomes angry whenever her sons misbehave, their relationship will suffer.

Exercise: Your Anger Cycle

Have you recently had an experience like Maria's? Can you identify your triggering event, negative thoughts, emotional responses, physical symptoms and behaviors?

Two Ways to Break the Cycle
Strategy #1: Challenge Your Thoughts

When you enter the anger cycle, you jump from a triggering event straight to negative thoughts, which in turn trigger your emotional response. If you can identify your negative thoughts and learn how to shut them down, you'll stand a good chance of breaking the cycle entirely. The key is to identify them and replace them with a more realistic, constructive view of the situation.

ANGER & YOUR THOUGHTS

When therapists work with angry clients, they sometimes focus on their client's cognitive distortions. Cognitive distortions are patterns of thinking that make a difficult situation worse. Distorted thinking can make even a minor inconvenience seem unbearable.

Here are the most common distortions and why they can fuel anger:

1. **Filtering**

    You focus on things someone else has done that annoy or anger you, overlook any good intentions they may have, and disregard positive memories.

    Example: "He insulted me! He's so rude."

2. **Overgeneralization**

    You judge everyone and everything in black-and-white terms. People who overgeneralize are fond of the words "always," "never," and "every."

    Example: "She never asks me what I'd like to do on the weekend."

3. **Blueprinting**

    You get angry at someone, then spend time daydreaming about how you will get revenge or "get even." Some people get distracted for hours dwelling on what they'd like to do to someone else.

Example: "I know precisely how I'm going to make her feel sorry for what she said. I'll ignore her tonight, and maybe tomorrow too!"

4. **Labeling**

   You focus on a single negative flaw or a few mistakes and give someone a "label" based on your judgment.

   Example: "He's a total idiot."

5. **Thresholding**

   You decide on an arbitrary standard or limit, and when someone exceeds or violates it, you get angry. You tell yourself that you "can't tolerate" their behavior and give yourself permission to get mad.

   Example: "I've given her two warnings already! That's enough—it's time to show her how angry I really am!"

6. **"Should-ing"**

   You insist that everyone behave in a particular way around you, or that they give you special treatment. When they don't live up to your expectations, you get angry.

   Example: "It's absolutely unacceptable that he's late to our coffee date."

7. **Blame**

    You don't try to understand your own role in the problem and choose to blame other people instead.

    Example: "It's all my mother's fault."

You can probably see why these thinking styles set you up to feel hurt, disappointed, frustrated, irritated, or furious. Negative thoughts cue negative emotions, which in turn trigger inappropriate behavior. They pop up so quickly, it's as though they are automatic. Some people call them "ANTs"—Automatic Negative Thoughts.

Exercise: Spotting Unhelpful Beliefs

Read the following beliefs. For each belief, decide whether it's an example of filtering, overgeneralization, blueprinting, labeling, thresholding, 'should'-ing, or blame.

- *It's all my boss's fault.*
- *My neighbor is a complete moron.*
- *I've warned the kids twice about the state of their room, the mess is totally unacceptable.*
- *My mother ought to go along with what I want.*
- *My friend has been late twice now; she's so inconsiderate.*
- *I'm going to get my revenge on him; he's in for it now!*
- *My neighbor always tries to make my mornings miserable.*

You'll find the answers at the bottom of the page.[1]

---

[1] [Answers: Blame, Labeling, Thresholding, Should-ing, Filtering, Blueprinting, Overgeneralization]

Working with Unhelpful Thoughts

You can do this with or without a notebook, but recording your thoughts makes it easier to work through the steps without losing focus. Some people also find that putting their thoughts down on the page makes them seem less overwhelming.

1. **Write down the thought.**

    Be specific. It doesn't matter if the thought is embarrassing or makes you feel uncomfortable. You don't have to show your notes to anyone else.

2. **Write down how you feel whenever you have this thought.**

    Again, go into as much detail as you can. Take a moment to pin down your emotions. Are you feeling furious, mildly irritated, or somewhere in between?

3. **Identify which distortion(s) you are using.**

    Are you overgeneralizing, filtering, labeling, should-ing, blaming, blueprinting, or thresholding?

4. **Write down a number between 1 and 10 to indicate how fully you accept this thought.**

    A score of 1 means you barely believe it, whereas a score of 10 means it is completely convincing.

5. **Identify a new, more helpful thought that will let you reframe the situation.**

    Ask yourself:[20]
    - What would I say to a friend in this situation?

- Do I have any evidence to support this thought? How do I know it's true?
- Is it helpful for me to hold onto this thought?
- Am I taking this too personally?
- Am I assuming the worst of someone else for no good reason?
- Will I care about this situation in a week, a month, a year? How important is it really?

Your new thought should be realistic. If it's positive, that's a bonus. Don't try to force yourself to feel optimistic about a bad situation.

6. **Write down a number between 1 and 10 to indicate how much you accept this new thought.**

   If it's less than 5, challenge yourself to come up with another replacement thought.

7. **Ask yourself, "How does holding this new thought make me feel?"**

   Hopefully, it will make you feel better. If not, go back to the beginning and repeat the steps.

   The first few times you try this exercise, it may take you several minutes. That's normal. Most of us aren't in the habit of slowing down and examining our thought processes. Eventually, you'll be so good at working with your distortions that you'll be able to identify them whenever they pop up.

Exercise: Challenging A Negative Thought

The next time you start getting angry, pause and take a moment to notice the thoughts going through your mind. Are you using any cognitive distortions? Next, follow the steps above to replace your thought with a healthier perspective that makes you feel better about the situation.

STRATEGY #2: LEARN TO COPE WITH YOUR EMOTIONS

You can break the cycle by learning how to cope with strong emotions. Remember, when your anger feels out of control, your emotional response dictates your behaviors. So, if you can pick up a few techniques that help you regain mastery over your feelings, you are less likely to lash out at others or turn your anger on yourself.

BREAKING THE LINK BETWEEN EMOTIONS & BEHAVIOR

If challenging your thoughts isn't working, you can still prevent yourself from lashing out at others by using simple, effective techniques to lower your stress levels the next time you feel attacked.

Try these strategies:

1. **Get some psychological distance from the situation**

    Pretend that the situation is happening to someone else. A little psychological distance helps you behave more rationally.[21]

2. **Do some deep breathing**

   It's a cliché, but deep breathing really does work to soothe your nervous system. Breathe in and out slowly and deeply, holding each breath for four to seven seconds. Deep breathing stimulates an area of the brain known as the breathing pacemaker. This pacemaker comprises around 3,000 brain cells situated in the medulla, an area of the brain responsible for maintaining basic bodily functions and reflexes.[22] When activated, these cells induce a feeling of relaxation.

3. **Ask for a 'time out' if you're around other people**

   If you're on the verge of doing or saying something you'll regret, excuse yourself for a few minutes. Take yourself off to another room or outside, do some deep breathing, and come back when you feel calmer.

4. **Get some physical activity**

   The chemicals your body releases when you feel angry give you a jolt of energy, which can make it hard to think clearly. Taking a quick walk around the block lowers your stress levels and triggers your body to release endorphins.[23] Endorphins, also known as "nature's painkillers," reduce tension and stabilize your mood.

5. **Change your posture and facial expression**

   You can trick your brain into feeling calmer or happier than you really are by changing your body language. The next time you feel angry, check in with your body. You'll probably find that you're clenching your fists and jaw or folding your arms. Take a deep breath and uncurl your fingers, drop your arms by your sides, and drop your shoulder muscles.

6. **Let yourself laugh**

   Watching or reading something funny won't solve your problems, but it can be an effective temporary distraction. Laughter releases tension and, just like exercise, boosts your endorphins. If you can't pull up a humorous video or article, recall something funny that happened to you in the past.

7. **Turn on some music that makes you happy**

   Listen to a song that lifts your mood and makes you think of happier times. It's impossible to feel angry for long if you focus on the beat and lyrics of a happy song you love. Tracks with a tempo of 60 to 80 beats per minute are most effective.[24]

Exercise: Pick A Playlist

Don't wait until you next feel angry to choose music that calms you down. Put together a playlist now, so that it's ready when you need it. Make it at least 30 minutes long.

SUMMARY

- When you break down an angry episode, you'll notice it follows a pattern: a trigger, negative thought, emotion, and behavior.
- Breaking the link between triggers and negative thoughts, and breaking the link between emotions and behaviors, can shut down your anger.
- Quick techniques you can use to handle feelings of anger include physical activity, self-distancing, and deep breathing.

CHAPTER 4:

UNDERSTANDING & HANDLING ANGER IN RELATIONSHIPS

In this chapter, you'll discover how anger follows a predictable cycle in romantic relationships, and how you can keep it from driving you and your partner apart. You'll learn some key communication skills that will empower you both. Most of the techniques and ideas in this section also apply to handling problems in family relationships and friendships.

THE CYCLE OF ANGER IN RELATIONSHIPS

Angry people often have angry relationships. Usually, one person feels mistreated or frustrated, which kick starts a destructive cycle that drags both partners down.

The cycle normally goes like this:[25]

- **Partner A becomes angry because they believe that Partner B has treated them badly.**
  This mistreatment—which can be actual or perceived—could be trivial or major. For example, Partner A might believe that Partner B has been

flirting with someone at work and feel angry as a result.

- **Partner A engages in negative, destructive behaviors.**
  Because Partner A doesn't know how to handle their own emotions or start a calm conversation with their partner, they resort to destructive behavior instead. They may use overt forms of aggression, such as shouting or passive-aggressive tactics like sulking.

- **Partner B notices Partner A's behaviors.**
  Unless they are willfully oblivious, Partner B will pick up on Partner A's anger. Partner B will feel attacked, blamed, and possibly rejected.

- **Partner B becomes angry at Partner A.**
  If they don't have the skills to start a constructive dialogue with Partner A, Partner B responds with their own anger.

The cycle continues. Over time, both partners may slip into a state of habitual anger. The underlying issues are never resolved. One or both partners might lash out, but neither knows how to reach a mutual understanding.

If this cycle continues long enough, both people can become resentful of one another. They may start believing that their relationship is doomed. They stop enjoying one another's company and may split up. Sometimes this is the best solution; not all relationships are destined to work out. However, many relationships could be saved if both partners take the time to master basic communication skills and simple anger management techniques.

Exercise: The Anger Cycle in Your Relationship

Think back to the last time you felt angry at your partner. How did both of you move through the anger cycle? What happened to make you or your partner so angry? Did you manage to resolve the issue, or is it still causing problems in your relationship?

HOW TO SHUT THE CYCLE DOWN BEFORE IT BEGINS

The good news is that the cycle isn't inevitable. If you learn how to communicate your wants and needs in a relationship and address problems as they arise, you can enjoy a more harmonious life together.

Try these strategies:

1. **Reframe your partner's behavior**

    Suppose your partner promised to cook dinner one evening. You come home from work and find your partner watching TV instead, with no sign that they are even thinking about making a meal. How would you respond? You could berate them for being lazy. Or you could take a passive-aggressive approach, perhaps by ignoring them and sighing as you start making your own dinner. Both responses would definitely let them know you are disappointed and angry.

    Alternatively, you could try a different tactic and reframe the situation. You could ask, "What would be a more charitable interpretation of their behavior here?" In this instance, you might say to yourself, "There's no evidence that they've forgotten completely. They might have lost track of the time, or maybe they were waiting until I got home so we could talk for a while before they start cooking."

How do you think you'd speak and act towards your partner if you chose to reframe their behavior like this? You'd probably be more patient, ask straightforward questions instead of berating them, and focus on the facts rather than starting a fight.

[Of course, some behaviors can't and shouldn't be reframed. If your partner is behaving in an abusive way, it's not helpful or safe to reframe their actions. Focus on keeping yourself safe instead.]

2. **Distance yourself from the situation**

   In the last chapter, you learned about self-distancing. Take a step back and imagine that one of your friends or relatives were in your situation. Watch the scenario play out as though it were happening to someone else instead. What would you advise them to do?

3. **Use constructive communication to resolve your differences instead of just expressing anger**

   This is the most important step. The best way to break the anger cycle is to start a mature, mutually beneficial conversation with your partner. Respectful conversations:

- Give all parties the chance to make their views known
- Are honest
- Come from a place of mutual compassion
- Are never abusive
- Can be difficult and draining, but allow both sides to work towards a solution

Here are a few things to keep in mind:

1. **Using insults and generalizations only makes things worse**

   Insulting someone puts them on the defensive. If your partner insults you, don't pay them back in kind. It's better to walk away completely than let yourself be drawn into a mud-slinging match.

2. **Shouting is never helpful**

   Shouting can feel cathartic, but it escalates conflict. It invites hostility and keeps your body in a state of high alert. Your partner will probably shout back, and both of you will feel worse.

3. **Seeking to understand, rather than persuade, is the best tactic**

   Are you more concerned with winning, or do you want to reach an understanding? If you treat every conversation like a battleground, your partner will soon realize that you don't actually want to work with them—you only want to be right. Put your ego to one side and concentrate on gathering information. Don't minimize your partner's feelings by telling them to "calm down," and don't imply they are overreacting.

4. **Planning for difficult conversations is a smart idea**

    It's OK to plan a conversation in advance. It might seem strange, but writing down the points you want to cover and even rehearsing how you will explain your point of view can be very helpful.

Exercise: Planning for a Sensitive Conversation

Are there any ongoing problems in your relationship? If you and your partner keep arguing about the same "hot button" topic over and over again, it's time to try a new approach. Instead of waiting for the subject to come up in conversation and then repeating your usual points, make some notes on how the issue makes you feel, what you'd like you and your partner to do differently, and a few ideas on how the two of you could work together to come up with solutions to your problems. Ask your partner when the two of you can discuss the issue. Using notes will help you structure the conversation and prevent you from getting overwhelmed.

5. **Giving each other time to talk, checking your understanding, then swapping roles lets you both feel heard**

    Decide who will speak first. Flip a coin if you can't decide. Set a timer for 3-5 minutes. The first speaker gets to talk, uninterrupted, while the timer is running. The listener's job is to do whatever it takes to keep themselves from butting in while trying to understand what their partner is saying.

When the speaker has finished, the listener paraphrases the main points to check that they've understood what was said. The partners then swap roles. Only after each person has had a chance to express their views do they work together to solve their problems. Trying to jump straight to the problem-solving stage won't work.

If you interrupt your partner when it's their turn to talk, apologize immediately and ask them to keep going. If your partner interrupts you when it's your turn to speak, pause the timer, calmly wait until they have finished, then say, "I'm going to talk again now. Please don't interrupt until the time is up." If they can't respect this boundary, take a time out and resume the conversation later.

6. **Use "I" statements when talking about your feelings**

   "I" statements are less confrontational than sentences that begin with "You," which often come across as aggressive or judgmental. Avoid starting sentences with "You always," "You never," or "You should." Instead, begin with a statement about the other person's behavior, then follow up by explaining how it makes you feel.

For example, instead of saying, "You never do your share of the housework!" it would be more constructive to say, "When you leave your dirty dishes in the sink every day for me to clean, I feel unappreciated."

Next, spell out what you want from the other person. Keep your requests reasonable and specific. To continue with the example above, you could say, "I would like you to clean up every other day because this means we are splitting the job equally."

7. **Notice patterns**[26]

   Good communication depends on both parties being willing to put in the necessary effort. If your partner doesn't want to cooperate, don't drive yourself crazy by holding onto the hope that their communication skills will improve.

   In some cases, you might even need to think about whether you want to continue with the relationship. For example, if you've been trying all the techniques in this chapter for several weeks, yet your partner seems uninterested in understanding your feelings or making positive changes, you need to realize that your wellbeing just isn't as important to them as theirs is to you.

8. **Don't make unfounded accusations**

   Before accusing your partner of doing something wrong, stop for a moment and ask yourself whether your suspicions are supported by evidence. A gut feeling or hunch doesn't count.

9. **Don't drag up the past**

    Unless it's directly relevant to whatever problems you're having in the present, leave the past where it belongs. Many couples get drawn into discussions and arguments about people and events that have no bearing on their current problems, which only makes it harder to tackle issues that affect them in the present.

10. **Don't use sarcasm**

    Sarcasm is a form of mockery, and mockery has no place in respectful conversations. It achieves nothing, aside from aggravating your partner. If you catch yourself making a sarcastic remark, apologize immediately.

11. **Watch your body language**

    Check that your words, tone of voice, and body language are in alignment. Keep your tone of voice steady, keep your arms and legs uncrossed, and avoid staring or using other hostile body language.

12. **Don't stonewall**

    Psychologist and relationship expert John Gottman has identified four signs that a relationship is in trouble: criticism, contempt, defensiveness, and stonewalling. To stonewall someone means to withdraw or shut down when they are trying to talk to you, and it isn't a healthy response to conflict.[27] Calling a timeout is a good idea if an argument is spiraling out of control or you aren't making any progress, but don't withdraw completely.

13. Agree on a trigger word

Choose a word your partner can use during an argument if they feel you are being unreasonably angry. When they use the word, it's time to take a breather.

Exercise: Do You Fight Fair?

Having read the list of "rules" for healthy communication, would you say you have any areas you need to work on? If you were to ask your partner, would they agree with you?

TIPS FOR DEALING WITH ANOTHER ANGRY PERSON

Communication can be hard work when you're dealing with a calm person. If your partner happens to be angry, it's even tougher. So far in this book, we've focused on strategies you can use to keep your anger under control, but what if your partner has similar struggles?

Here's what to do if you're trying to talk to an angry person:

1. Let them run out of steam

If someone has worked him/herself up into a fit of rage, they won't be able to process anything you say until they have finished making their point. Bite your tongue and let them talk. If you interrupt, they will feel disrespected.

2. **Make safety your first priority**

   Nothing is more important than your personal safety. If someone makes you feel unsafe, get away as soon as possible. If it's absolutely essential that you have a discussion with them, you could ask an independent third party to stay in the room at all times, hold the discussion in a safe public place, or only engage with them on the phone.

3. **Try not to take their words personally**

   Other people might label you, but you don't have to accept their judgments. It doesn't matter if they yell, "You're an idiot!" several times in a row—it still isn't true. Remind yourself that it isn't worth getting angry at a lie.

4. **If their anger is justified, show you understand why they are upset**

   Angry people often feel mistreated, short-changed, humiliated, or disappointed. If you can show empathy and validate their emotions, they are more likely to calm down. When they have stopped talking, paraphrase their words back to them and finish with, "Have I understood that correctly?"

Note that a person can feel angry for a good reason but express it in a completely inappropriate way. For example, suppose you agree to have coffee with a friend one morning, but then forget about it. It wouldn't be unreasonable for your friend to feel angry when you don't show up.

However, if they call you and subject you to verbal abuse, their response is unjustified.

In these cases, separate the event and the response. You can then apologize for your part in the incident, but also let the other person know that you will not tolerate their inappropriate anger.

5. **Ask what they want you to do next**

    This question can throw people off guard. Sometimes, angry people are so caught up in their feelings that they don't actually know what they want from others. Offer them the chance to take a few minutes or hours away to decide what they want to happen next. They might realize that the only thing they wanted to do was rant and let their feelings out.

6. **Stay cool**

    Do your best to act calm, even if you are raging on the inside. If you return their rage, the situation will only escalate. By keeping your voice low and your body language non-confrontational, you'll encourage them to calm down. Human beings tend to match or "mirror" one another.[28] By subtly modeling what calm behavior looks like, you might take the edge off their anger. Under no circumstances should you tell them to "calm down" or "chill out"—that will make them feel belittled, which in turn will feed their fury.

Exercise: How Will These Tips Change Your Relationship?

Think back to the last time you had an argument with another angry person. Imagine if you had used the six strategies above. How would the scenario have played out differently? If you were to adopt them in all your future discussions, what do you think will happen to your relationship?

PROBLEM-SOLVING WITH A PARTNER

Once you've both calmed down and explained things from your perspective, you can start to address any underlying problems. Begin by affirming that you love one another and want to work together as a team. In the heat of an argument, it's easy to forget that you and your partner are on the same side. Pausing in the middle of a tense discussion and reminding them how much you love them can ease the tension.

Next, identify the problem. Narrow your focus until you can sum up the issue in a single sentence. For example, "We need to both take responsibility for chores around the house so that neither of us feels over-burdened or resentful." If you have multiple problems to tackle, take them one at a time. Keep the discussion going until you reach a mutual agreement.

The next step is to think of potential solutions. You can do this together or draw up separate lists. Give yourself plenty of time; your first (or second) idea won't necessarily be your best.

If one or both of you feel overwhelmed, take a few hours or days apart to think through your options. Don't be afraid to think creatively and come up with solutions that seem a little bit quirky or unconventional. Place your lists side by side and compare suggestions. Before you start weighing the pros and cons of each, ask your partner to agree that neither of you will be unkind or dismissive of the other's solutions.

You might be pleasantly surprised to find that the items on your lists match. If not, move forward with an open mind. Ask your partner to explain their perspective if their ideas don't make sense to you.

When deciding on a solution, be prepared to compromise. No one gets to have things their way all the time in relationships. Adopt an attitude of compassionate curiosity. If your partner is arguing in favor of a solution that seems strange or inappropriate, try to assume the best; they probably aren't out to make your life difficult.

When You're Stuck

Self-help can rescue relationships, but sometimes you may need to bring in a professional. If you've been trying the techniques in this chapter for several weeks but haven't noticed any improvements, consider seeing a therapist to help you get back on track. If your partner doesn't show any motivation to improve the relationship, this is a big red flag. You can't, and shouldn't, be solely responsible for saving your relationship.

If there is abuse in your relationship, or your partner has disengaged and refuses to talk about your problems, it's a good idea to reach out to a couples' therapist with experience in this area. You can visit a relationship therapist alone if your partner doesn't want to attend.

Summary

- It is normal for one or both people in a relationship to get angry, but anger can develop into a vicious cycle if it isn't addressed properly.
- Reframing your partner's behavior, distancing yourself from the situation, learning some basic communication skills, and mastering the art of problem-solving will ease tension in your relationship.
- Preparing in advance for difficult conversations makes it easier to resolve your issues.
- If your partner is abusive, refuses to engage with you, or makes you feel unsafe, seek professional support.

CHAPTER 5:

HOW TO GROW YOUR EMOTIONAL INTELLIGENCE

So far, we've focused on how to identify and work with your anger. In this chapter, we're going to step back and take a broader view. We're going to think about how anger is linked with other emotions, how to release toxic shame, and why growing your emotional intelligence will help you live a calmer life.

Is Your Anger a Sign of a Deeper Problem?

Sometimes, anger has an obvious cause. For instance, if someone cuts you off in traffic, it makes sense that you'd be mad. The other driver has violated the rules of the road and possibly put you and others in danger. If your partner forgets your birthday and you interpret it as a sign they don't care about you, then it's natural you'd feel upset and angry.

However, anger is often a cover for disappointment, fear, and other emotions. When you work on taking control over your anger, you might find they start to bubble up to the surface. For example, if you have been feeling angry with your partner because they keep canceling your plans in favor of hanging out with their friends instead, your anger might be mixed with a fear of rejection or deep sadness that your partner prefers the company of other people.

ANGER & SHAME

According to psychologist Andrea Brandt, anger can be a cover for shame.[29] Shame is often used as another term for guilt, but they are not the same. Guilt is a feeling you experience when you've done something wrong, whereas shame is a sense that you are a bad person. For example, if you accidentally break your partner's favorite mug and hide the pieces to avoid being held responsible, you may feel guilty. If your partner finds out and shouts at you, telling you that you are a horrible liar and deserve to feel bad about yourself, you might feel shame.

Shame is painful. It can also come mixed with other emotions and make them feel more intense. You can feel shame alongside disgust, sadness, and even enjoyment. Shame is a pervasive emotion that can stick around for a long time. Some people feel ashamed of how they've acted in the past, but it's also possible to feel shame when someone else hurts you. For example, abused children often grow up with a sense of shame even though they are in no way to blame for their abuser's actions.

When you feel ashamed of yourself, you are more sensitive to criticism than other people, because you already tend to see yourself as weaker or inferior to others. Shame can be a major anger trigger because getting mad can feel safer than looking at your weaknesses and fears. In other words, irritation and rage are great diversionary tactics.[30] Shame makes us feel small and threatened, and anger can be an effective defense.

A single event can be enough to instill a sense of shame that lasts for decades. Let's look at an example:

William is a high-spirited four-year-old boy who enjoys playing outside. One afternoon, he comes in from the yard and into the house. He tramples mud all over the living room and hallway. His mother is furious. She yells, "Why are you so muddy? You are a wretched child! You just want to make my life difficult! Now, help me clean up this mess!" Young William feels scared and ashamed.

Thirty years later, William is in the kitchen reading the newspaper and drinking a cup of coffee. His wife, Beth, comes home with several bags of groceries. After Beth has finished putting away the groceries, she starts to think about the rest of her to-do list for the day. The house needs a deep clean. She asks William, "Would you please clean the garage today? The floor is dirty from where you've been working on your motorbike."

William quickly gets annoyed. Although Beth has made a polite request, he jumps to the conclusion that she is attacking him for being lazy, messy, and in some way not good enough. He immediately launches into a long tirade about how many hours he works each week and how he's "so sorry" for being "such a terrible husband."

In this example, William felt shame as a child because his mother got angry when he made a mess. As an adult, that old feeling of shame is triggered whenever his wife asks him to clean up. William hasn't ever worked through his old feelings of shame or his troubled relationship with his mother. As a result, he is hypersensitive to even low-level criticism.

As a young child, he didn't have the maturity to slow down and think to himself, "My mother says I am wretched. What is the evidence for and against this claim? How can I replace it with a more productive, balanced perspective?" His only choice was to accept that whatever his mother said was true. Fortunately, as an adult, he can choose to think about his experiences in a new light.

How to Heal Shame

Shame thrives in secrecy. Sharing your story with someone safe can be enormously liberating. Carrying a secret weighs you down and makes you feel isolated. Healing from shame is an important part of your anger management journey.

There are several ways to offload shame. Your first option is to pick an empathetic friend or family member you can trust. Ask them whether they would mind if you shared a personal story with them, and request that they keep it to themselves. Give as much or as little detail as you like. You may be surprised to learn that they have a similar story to tell. Lots of us grow up thinking that no one else has ever felt the same way, but deep-seated shame is more common than you might think.

Some people prefer to talk to a mental health professional, usually a therapist. Because therapists are neutral third parties and are bound by confidentiality agreements, you don't have to worry that they will tell anyone you know. If you would prefer talking to someone anonymous, there are lots of 24/7 hotlines and online chat services staffed by trained volunteers.

Finally, if you would rather work through your shame alone, you could try journaling. Whether you prefer to write or type, getting your story down on the page is healing.

Exercise: Journaling About Shame

Write a factual account of the event or events that caused you to feel shame. Where were you? Who was there? What happened? Walk through the memory, step by step. If you feel overwhelmed, take a break. Journaling can also be a great addition to therapy. If you are seeing a therapist and feel comfortable sharing your writing, consider taking your journal to your next session.

Self-forgiveness is another important tool for shedding shame. Later in this book, you'll learn how to move past old mistakes.

Anger & Sadness

Some people are raised to believe that expressing sadness is a form of weakness and that you will earn more respect if you get angry instead. If you have lost something or someone important to you, it's natural and normal to feel sad. Sadness leads to feelings of vulnerability, which can be uncomfortable. If you can't or won't acknowledge your sadness, it can take the form of anger. Just as anger can be a shield against shame, it can also feel safer than admitting to yourself or others that you feel sad.

Anger & Anxiety

Anxiety often takes the form of a fear that events are sliding out of your control. If you are worried that you can't take charge of your own life, you might become easily angered, especially if you don't think other people are giving you the help you deserve. You also may be angry at yourself for being anxious and worried in the first place. Fear is also linked to jealousy, which is a fear of loss. We'll come back to the problem of jealousy in Chapter 9.

Shame, sadness, and anxiety feel overwhelming if you don't have the right tools to deal with them. The good news is that by learning more about how emotions work and how you can regulate your own feelings, you will no longer have to resort to using anger as a coping mechanism.

What is Emotional Intelligence & Why is it Helpful?

Emotional intelligence, also known as EI, is a set of skills that enables you to manage emotions.

The three psychologists who first defined EI describe it like this:

> "Emotional intelligence refers to an ability to recognize the meanings of emotion and their

relationships, and to reason and problem-solve on the basis of them. Emotional intelligence is involved in the capacity to perceive emotions, assimilate emotion-related feelings, understand the information of those emotions, and manage them (Mayer, Caruso & Salovey, 1999, p. 267)."[31]

If we break EI down further, we can see that it's made up of several traits and skills. These include:

1. **Self-awareness**

    Self-awareness grants you an ability to recognize emotions, both positive and negative, as they pop up in your daily life. Self-aware people don't shy away from unpalatable emotions. They automatically tune into their bodies and minds to get a reading on how they truly feel.

    Emotionally intelligent people can reason about their emotions. For instance, suppose someone who has high EI realizes they feel jealous when their partner goes away on a work trip, even though there is no logical reason to suspect that their partner is cheating or lying to them. They would tell themselves that it's OK to feel a little insecure from time to time, but there's no need to worry unless they have a good reason to suspect that their partner is cheating on them.

2. **Self-regulation**

   Self-regulation is the ability to choose coping strategies that help you work through negative emotions. We've already covered some self-regulation techniques in this book, such as reframing a situation, distancing yourself from a problem, and doing some exercise.

   People who score high on measures of self-regulation stick to their moral codes and standards even when under pressure; they don't take shortcuts that would leave them feeling guilty or inadequate later on. They are open to learning new techniques for regulating their emotions and always take responsibility for their own feelings. They know how to overcome resistance to change, and they stay strong in the face of setbacks.

3. **Ability to recognize emotions in other people**

   For a long time, psychologists thought there were six facial expressions found in all cultures—happiness, sadness, surprise, fear, disgust, and anger. Recent research has shown this isn't necessarily the case. There are differences between cultures in how people express emotions.[32] However, we can all practice "reading" other people, whatever their background. People with well-developed emotional intelligence are quick to pick up on other people's feelings and offer their support when appropriate.

4. **Empathy**
   Empathy is the ability to put yourself in someone else's position in order to understand their emotions and actions. Empathy isn't the same as pity or sympathy, which is a feeling of compassion or concern for someone in difficulty.

WHY IS EI HELPFUL FOR ANGER PROBLEMS?

By growing your EI, you will learn how to handle challenging feelings. By facing them as and when they crop up, you are less likely to fall back on using anger as a shield or coping mechanism.

Try these strategies to improve your EI:

1. **Keep a journal**
   Journaling is a great way to release tension, which can ease anger or frustration in the short-term. It helps you grow your self-knowledge. Regularly writing about your feelings helps you identify patterns in how you react to the world around you. Armed with this information, you can then make informed decisions about how you want to handle emotionally charged situations in the future.

   For example, if you notice that you tend to feel low on Friday evenings, you could zone in on that pattern and explore what might be going on. Perhaps you don't feel as though you have enough to do on the weekends, or maybe you are lonely. Or perhaps you find yourself getting angry on Monday mornings, which just so happen to be when you have a weekly check-in with your annoying boss. Stay curious about your emotions. They have much to teach you.

2. **Read & watch stories with complicated characters**

    Immersing yourself in complex storylines with well-developed characters challenges you to think about what they are thinking and feeling, which is good training for the real world. The next time you become engrossed in a book or film, ask yourself why and how the characters have grabbed your imagination. What are their motivations? Can you tell what they are thinking before they share what's on their minds?[33]

3. **Ask questions**

    When was the last time you asked your loved ones how they were feeling, and then gave them all the time they needed to respond? When life gets busy, it's easier to stick with trivial conversations. We might say "I hope you're doing well" or "How are you today?" without really expecting or wanting a reply.

    Over the coming week, ask at least three people how they've been feeling recently. Pick the right moment—perhaps over coffee or during a phone call when you both have at least ten minutes to chat. So many of us keep our problems all to ourselves because even those closest to us don't have time to slow down and listen. They might be relieved to have the opportunity to talk about something that's been bothering them. If they ask similar questions in return, be honest. Let yourself be vulnerable. Taking your conversations to the next level forces you to develop your emotional literacy and face up to how you're really feeling.

4. **Read about emotions & grow your vocabulary**

   How are you feeling right now? Emotions are complex. It can be hard to put how you feel into words. Reading about emotions will help you grow your "feelings vocabulary," which in turn will help you express yourself. This can make a big difference when it comes to letting others know how you feel.[34]

Exercise: Putting Words to Your Emotions

Get a pen and a piece of paper. Write down as many words related to feelings as you can. Aim for at least 50, more if you can think of them. Go to Google and search for "list of feelings words." You'll be surprised at how many words and phrases there are in the English language you can use to describe your emotions.

5. **Ask Yourself, "What would I want someone else to do?"**

   It's not always easy to know what to do or say when someone else gets upset or mad. Next time you're in this situation, ask yourself how you'd want someone else to respond. Would you want them to acknowledge your problem, offer a solution, or distract you?

6. **Ask Yourself, "What worked the last time I had this feeling?"**

    People high in EI make a conscious choice to handle their emotions. For example, when they notice the early signs of stress, they say to themselves, "OK, I need to calm down. What constructive thing can I do to feel better in this moment?" By contrast, someone low in EI gets swept up in their feelings, and they don't learn from the past. Even if they do find a way to make themselves feel better, they don't remember to use it next time around. You can keep a record of what helps you cope with difficult feelings in your journal.

7. **Get some honest feedback**

    We aren't always the best judges of our own abilities. Getting input from trusted relatives, friends, and colleagues can help you improve your EI by highlighting your strengths and weaknesses. Only 10-15% of us have a high level of self-awareness, and those in the highest positions in a company are most likely to overestimate their abilities. This may be because the more senior your position, the fewer people you have to give you truthful, useful feedback.[35]

"How emotionally intelligent do you think I am?" is a big question, so focus on specific skills instead. Ask, "How well do you think I respond to tough situations?" or "How good would you say I am at handling conflict?"

As an angry or sensitive person, you might not get honest feedback because everyone may be afraid of hurting your feelings. That's OK. As you grow your EI, your loved ones will start to trust in your ability to handle constructive criticism. You might also get spontaneous compliments, like "You've been so much calmer lately! I used to have to walk on eggshells around you, but now it's so much easier to talk to you." These comments are a great sign that you have made progress.[36]

Summary

- Anger can be an uncomplicated response to a person or situation, but anger is often mixed up with other challenging emotions.
- Shame, fear, and sadness are common anger triggers for people who cannot or will not acknowledge, and work with, their feelings.
- Growing your emotional intelligence will improve your ability to cope with difficult feelings, which in turn will make it easier to keep your anger and frustration under control.
- Adopting an attitude of curiosity, journaling, and watching shows with complex characters can help to develop your EI.
- If possible, ask people you trust to give their opinion on your EI and social skills.

CHAPTER 6:

MINDFULNESS FOR ANGER MANAGEMENT

Mindful people are not immune to anger. They get irritated, stressed, and upset. However, they don't let their feelings hijack their reasoning. They take a moment to notice their emotions, then they decide to let them go. In this chapter, we're going to look at how living a more mindful life will help grow your EI and cope with anger.

What Is Mindfulness?

Harvard psychologists Matthew Killingsworth and Daniel Gilbert, who have carried out research into mindfulness, believe that the average person spends 46.7% of their day in a state of distraction. We tend to think about the past, the future, and hypothetical situations instead of the task at hand. In a paper they published on the subject, the authors concluded, "our mental lives are pervaded, to a remarkable degree, by the non-present."[37] They also found that mindful people were typically happier than those with wandering thoughts.

Mindful people do not get sucked into rumination or worry. They have to deal with the same challenges as everyone else, but they don't suffer any more than is necessary. Being mindful isn't about emptying your head of all thoughts, which isn't a realistic goal anyway. Mindfulness entails recognizing and labeling whatever you are thinking or feeling, accepting it, and making a conscious choice to react in a way that services your own interests.

Mindfulness & Meditation

"Mindfulness" and "meditation" are often used interchangeably, but they are not the same. Meditation normally refers to a formal practice, usually seated, that entails focusing on a particular sound, mantra, idea, mental image, or other "anchor."[38] Mindfulness isn't a practice, but a state. You can be mindful anywhere—during meditation, while waiting in line at the grocery store, at work, and even during an argument.

Exercise: How Mindful Are You?

Put this book down for a moment and watch your thoughts for a minute or so. What's going through your mind? Are you wholly focused on the here and now, or is your mind chattering away? Are you worrying about anything?

Why Is Mindfulness Helpful for Anger Management?

As we discussed earlier in this book, it's not what happens to us that dictates our emotional reactions, but how we interpret the events in our lives. For example, if a colleague is late to a meeting, you will feel angry if you assume that they are disrespecting you. But if you tell yourself that everyone is late from time to time and that they probably aren't deliberately trying to make your life difficult, you won't feel quite so annoyed.

When you live mindfully, you can slow down and notice your unhelpful thoughts before they hijack your reactions. Instead of jumping to conclusions, you can become aware of how you are processing the situation and then choose to react in a more constructive way.

Mindfulness also helps you identify the physical sensations of anger, which is a cue to take a step back from the situation. For example, suppose you are irritated by someone else's behavior and your heart begins to pound in your chest. If you are being mindful, you can tune in to your body and notice that your heart rate has started to climb. You would then pause and choose an anger management strategy.

GETTING STARTED WITH MINDFULNESS: THREE PRACTICES

Mindfulness Practice #1: Body Scanning

This classic exercise is a great way to get into mindfulness. It gives you a chance to practice remaining in the moment and helps you get back in touch with your body. Lots of us live in our heads, ignoring or even disconnecting from our bodily sensations. Practiced regularly, body scanning will help you feel more comfortable in your own skin.[39]

- Lie or sit down somewhere comfortable. If you're tired, it's best to do the exercise seated. Otherwise, you may fall asleep.
- Close your eyes.
- Inhale. Feel the air enter your lungs. Exhale slowly.
- Turn your attention to your feet. How do they feel? Heavy? Light? Warm, cold, or somewhere in between? Can you detect any other sensations, such as buzzing, tingling, or itching? What do your feet feel like against the floor or bed?
- Slowly shift your awareness to your calves. Again, what sensations do you notice?
- Keep shifting your awareness upwards, slowly "scanning" your entire body. If your attention wanders, gently bring it back to your body and continue the exercise.
- Finish by scanning the muscles around your temples. Take your time. Ten to fifteen minutes is ideal, but you can keep going longer if you wish.
- When you've finished scanning, take another mindful breath. Slowly open your eyes.

Mindfulness Practice #2: Thoughts as Clouds

Do you feel overwhelmed by your internal chatter? Does your mind race so fast you can barely keep up? If so, this exercise is perfect for you. You will learn that every thought is transient; there's always another one ready to take its place.

- Lie down or sit somewhere comfortable.
- Close your eyes.

- Observe your thoughts. Your brain will come up with assorted thoughts and images. When you slow down and pay attention to your mind, you'll be surprised how scattered it is.
- Every time a new thought pops up, picture it as a cloud against a vast, blue sky.
- Watch the clouds float through the sky and away into the distance.
- Do this for five minutes.

Notice that you don't need to react to every thought and feeling. This is a valuable lesson if you struggle to manage your anger. It's OK to let thoughts go. In fact, it's the smartest way to reduce your suffering and stop ruminating about the things that make you mad.

Mindfulness Practice #3: Identifying Other Feelings

This practice helps you look more closely at your anger and discover whether it's masking any other emotions.[40]

- Stand with your feet shoulder-width apart.
- Notice how the floor feels beneath your feet. Remind yourself that the floor is secure and steady; it will support you.
- Check your posture. Stand up straight, with your shoulders back.
- Take a few deep breaths.
- Rub your shoulders, the back of your neck, and your arms. Pay attention to the sensations.

- Call to mind the event or person that made you feel angry.
- Say, "I am mad" or "I am angry." Say it several times, varying your volume and pitch. Each time, notice how the sensations in your body change.
- Identify and name other feelings, such as sadness, frustration, or fear.
- Soften your muscles and take a few more deep breaths.

Practice Makes Perfect: How Mindfulness Changes Your Brain

You've probably heard the old cliché, "You can't teach an old dog new tricks." This may be true for dogs, but it doesn't apply to humans. Our brains are plastic, which means we can and do adapt our behaviors over the course of our lives. As we learn new skills, the neural pathways in our brains change. The more often we practice a particular behavior, the stronger those pathways become. This means that anyone can train him/herself to become more mindful.[41]

Mindfulness takes practice. Think of it as a long-term anger management technique. Try these exercises when you are feeling calm. Repeat them several times each week, until being mindful becomes second nature. When you get angry, you won't have to walk yourself through the exercises step-by-step. You'll already know what to do and how to benefit from them.

Use Your Senses: Making Mindfulness a Part of Everyday Life

If you don't have the time or inclination to do the exercises above, you can still benefit from mindfulness. The easiest way to lead a more mindful life is to tune into your senses whenever you get the chance. When you are fully focused on smelling, tasting, touching, hearing or seeing something, you are grounding yourself in the present.

Try eating a meal or snack in a mindful way. When you take a bite, pay close attention to how the food feels in your mouth. Is it warm or cool? Chewy or smooth? Is it bitter, sweet, or salty? Stick a small note on your desk or in your wallet that says "TUNE IN." Every time you read the note, take a 30-second mindfulness break.

The RAIN Technique

RAIN is an easy-to-recall acronym you can use to give yourself a mindfulness boost, whatever the situation.

The next time you feel your temper rising, remember:[42]

1. **Recognition**

    Recognize that you have become angry. Pause for a moment before you act. Name your emotions.

2. **Acceptance**

    Accept how you feel. There is no need to suppress your anger. Strong emotions can feel scary, but they can't hurt you. Tell yourself, "At this moment in time, I feel angry."

3. **Investigation**

    Investigate what is going on in your body and mind. What thoughts are going through your head? How does your body feel? Are you tense, fidgety, or ready to fight? Try not to judge yourself.

4. **Non-identification**

    However strong your feelings are, they do not define you. You are more than your rage or annoyance. Emotions aren't static. They come and go throughout the day. You don't have to latch onto your feelings or analyze them; they simply "are." This is perhaps the most important lesson of all. Anger and other uncomfortable feelings are part of life, but they always pass.

Summary

- To be mindful is to live in the present.
- Mindfulness needs to be cultivated; by default, our thoughts tend to wander.
- Meditation is one way to practice mindfulness, but it isn't the only path to it.
- Mindfulness is a powerful anger management tool, as it puts you in touch with your emotions.
- Popular mindfulness exercises include body scanning and treating your thoughts like passing clouds.
- Anyone can learn to be mindful because our brains are plastic.

- Remember the acronym RAIN: Recognize, Accept, Investigate, Non-identification.
- To get the most from your mindfulness practices, repeat them several times each week.

CHAPTER 7:

FORGIVING OTHERS & LETTING GO OF GRUDGES

So far, we've talked about how to deal with anger in the present. But what about old grudges and resentments that still make you angry today? In this chapter, you'll learn how to work through the past and move on.

WHY GRUDGES ARE A PROBLEM

We've all been treated unfairly. Injustice is a fact of life. It's normal to feel occasional flashes of resentment when you think about people who have betrayed or abused you. But cultivating a grudge that keeps you locked in a state of anger for years isn't healthy.

Here's why:

1. **Grudges eat up your energy**

   How many minutes, hours, or even days have you spent ruminating about the past or fantasizing about revenge scenarios? Did it help? Perhaps you've found it cathartic to think about how you would humiliate someone who hurt you, but is it really the best use of your time? Probably not. Think of what you could do with that mental energy if you choose to move on from your grudge.

2. **Grudges make you cynical and distrustful**

   As you already know, your thoughts shape your emotions. If you focus on everything that's wrong with your life and in the world, your mood will take a nosedive. Think of the happiest, most well-adjusted people you know. Do they carry grudges and nurse their resentment? In general, positive people like to keep moving. They enjoy looking forward, not backward.

3. **If you keep talking about your old hurts and resentment, your relationships will suffer**

   Your friends and family don't want to hear you complain incessantly about your past. It's fine to ask for love and support when life gets tough, but rehashing the same events over and over again is destructive.

4. **Holding onto grudges makes you a target for toxic people**

   There is some truth to the saying, "birds of a feather flock together." If you want to attract well-balanced people into your life, you need to let go of resentment. Otherwise, you'll attract other people who can't leave the past behind. If you think of yourself as a victim, narcissists and other predators will pick up on your insecurities and latch onto you.

5. **Grudges don't undo what happened**

    No matter how much you dwell on the past, nothing can change it. With this in mind, why bother over-analyzing what happened days, months, years, or even decades ago? Would you advise someone else to obsess about past events, or would you gently tell them that they are wasting their time?

6. **You don't need your grudge**

    Part of you may hold onto your anger and hurt because you think it will protect you. For example, you might think that being angry and cynical will stop you from getting too close to others, which in turn will protect you from the pain of rejection. Or maybe you worry that other people will take advantage of you, and holding onto your pain means you won't be caught with your guard down.

    However, you don't need to hold onto the past to protect yourself in the present and future. You can set boundaries and make intelligent choices for yourself. You can learn from the past without being enslaved to it, and you can forgive someone without making yourself vulnerable. It's time to have a little faith in yourself.

    The idea that your grudge will somehow shield you from further pain is a form of magical thinking. Whether you choose to look forward or backward, life will still throw you a few curveballs.

To live well, you need to develop healthy coping strategies that will empower you to face problems with courage and dignity. The first step is to forgive those who have hurt you.

What is Forgiveness?

Forgiving someone does not mean you approve of what they did. Neither does it mean you have decided to forget about it. To forgive someone is to decide that you are no longer going to give their actions the power to hurt you.[43] When you have forgiven someone, any reminder of what they did no longer makes you feel angry.

Unfortunately, giving up a grudge is hard. Here's why:

1. **Grudges can become part of your identity**

    A grudge can be comforting. It can be validating to feel as though someone has wronged you. If you've been thinking of yourself as a victim for months, years, or even decades, it will be difficult to let go of your grudge. Without your resentment and rumination, you might not know who you are or what to focus on instead.

2. **Giving up a grudge requires work**

    Humans have a tendency to take the easy route. Letting go of the past is healing, but it's tough. You will have to revisit what happened, which can be uncomfortable or upsetting.

3. **Giving up a grudge feels as though you've let someone else "get away with it"**
   When you realize that feeling mad at someone is more painful for you than it is for them, you'll be one step closer to forgiveness. Consider this: Does the person who hurt you actually benefit if you privately decide to forgive them? In all probability, they don't know (or care) how you are feeling right now. Why not set yourself free by making the choice to move forward?

Here's a step-by-step guide to releasing resentment:

1. **Get the grudge down on paper**
   What, exactly, did the other person do that still makes you so mad? Be specific. If they have hurt you on several occasions, or in lots of different ways, make a detailed list of everything they've done wrong.

2. **Decide whether you should work on your grudge alone or seek professional help**
   Most of the time, you'll be able to work on forgiveness and releasing your resentment by yourself. But if you have experienced any kind of trauma connected with the event, or if the other person was abusive in a way that still makes you feel afraid, it's better to work with a therapist.

3. **Put yourself in the other person's position**
   Humans are complicated. Sometimes, we don't even know the motives behind our own behaviors.

Pretend that you have swapped bodies with the other person. Travel back in time to the moment they offended or wronged you. What might have been going through their mind?

Remember, you don't have to excuse their actions.[44] You can forgive someone while knowing that they did something bad. But sometimes, having an explanation can be healing. For example, did the other person pick up their bad behaviors or poor social skills from their family of origin? Were they going through a particularly stressful time when they mistreated you?

4. **Ask yourself whether holding onto your grudge has been helping or hurting you**

   On balance, is it in your best interests to keep nurturing your grudge? Has your resentment been holding you back in any areas of your life? For example, have you been reluctant to go on dates because you are still obsessed with someone who hurt you in a past relationship? You'll have more success in moving on if you can imagine what you will gain. What would it be like to be free of resentment?

5. **Write your own story**

   Combine your account of what happened with your list of reasons why the other person chose to act as they did. Write out a narrative that helps you make sense of the situation.

For example:

Three years ago, my best friend had an affair with the woman I was dating at the time. I only found out because an anonymous source sent me an email. I had to end my relationship, which I thought was going well, and I knew I could never trust my best friend again. After a big fight, we stopped speaking and I cut all contact with him. I was devastated and furious because I lost both a romantic partner and one of my closest pals. At the time, my friend was in a bad place. His job was on the line, and he was fighting with his wife about their teenage son, who was in trouble with the law. There is no excuse for what he did, but I think all the stress in his life—which I knew made him feel overwhelmed and scared—made him more likely to look for a distraction anywhere he could find it.

6. **Try to find the positives in the situation**

   No one enjoys being treated badly, but you can find some sense of meaning in life's trials and setbacks. For example, if a friend betrayed you, perhaps the experience has made you an excellent friend who always keeps other peoples' secrets. Or maybe your experience has given you valuable insight into how toxic relationships work, and you've been able to support other people with similar problems.

7. **Try saying "I forgive you" out loud**

   Say, "[Name], I forgive you." How did it feel? Perhaps it seems impossible to get the words out. That's OK. There's no rush. You can forgive the other person when you're ready. If you feel overwhelmed by this process, wait a few days and work through the steps again. Give yourself lots of praise for getting this far. Forgiveness work requires the kind of emotional strength that most people never bother to develop.

SELF-FORGIVENESS

Perhaps you can forgive others, but can't seem to forgive yourself? You aren't alone. Many of us have a harsh inner critic that tells us that we've messed up, that we are "bad," and so on. This voice isn't helpful. It holds you back from reaching your full potential because you become scared of making any more mistakes.

Adapt the seven steps listed above. Write down what you did and how your actions affected you and others. Next, think about your situation at the time and make a list of all the factors that resulted in your poor decision-making. Write out your personal story using neutral language. Decide whether obsessing over your past is helping you (it isn't!), and then make a conscious decision to let go of the past. Ask yourself whether you have learned any lessons from your experience and how you can avoid making the same mistakes again.

Finally, decide what you want to happen next.[45] Perhaps working through your emotions is enough, but you might want to ask someone else for forgiveness. Before you go ahead, ask yourself whether the other person is likely to appreciate your apology. Are you saying "sorry" because you think they'd want to hear it, or are you looking for closure for yourself? Be honest. If your only motive is to clear your own conscience, it may be best to work on self-forgiveness by yourself.

How to Ask Forgiveness

If you want to ask forgiveness, start with a sincere apology. Before you say "sorry," make sure you really mean it. No apology is better than an insincere apology. "I'm sorry you feel that way" or "I'm sorry it's come to this" isn't an apology. "I did something wrong, and I'm sorry" or "I shouldn't have done that, and I apologize" is much better.

Be willing to be corrected. The other person might have a different perspective on what happened. Place your ego to one side and don't assume that your version is objectively correct. We all have our biases; it's quite possible that neither of you is entirely right or wrong. What's important is that you give the person you hurt an opportunity to tell you how they feel.

No one owes you their forgiveness. This is one of life's toughest lessons. You can acknowledge where you went wrong, say sorry, and try to make amends, but the other party is under no obligation to forgive you.

Developing Compassion

When you develop compassion for yourself and others, your life will become easier. You won't waste precious time and energy making judgments or holding grudges.

Compassionate people realize that we are all imperfect beings living in an imperfect world. We have all been hurt, and we are all vulnerable.

Try these strategies to develop your empathy and see the world through other peoples' eyes:[46]

1. **Drop the criticism**

    Humans are imperfect creatures, and they often make mistakes. If you have a naturally critical or pedantic personality, are you spending too much time dwelling on their weaknesses, which will make you and everyone else miserable? Challenge yourself to see the good in others instead. Every time someone annoys you, think of one trait or achievement of theirs you admire. Before you criticize someone, ask yourself whether your feedback is really necessary.

2. **Bond with others**

    Even if you consider yourself very introverted, social isolation isn't good for your mental health. Spending time with people is the first step in developing meaningful relationships, which is the best way to practice appreciating and bonding with others. This week, call up a friend or relative and invite them to share a hobby or activity.

3. **The compassion chair**

    The next time someone's behavior upsets or angers you, try a role-playing exercise. Place two chairs next to one another. One chair represents your perspective. The other represents that of the other person.

Sit in the first chair and think about the situation from your perspective. How are you feeling? What questions do you have for the other person? Sit in the other chair and respond on their behalf. This requires imagination and patience, but it can help you empathize with them.

You can use a variation of this exercise to develop compassion toward yourself. When you sit in the first chair, speak as yourself. When you move to the second chair, play the part of a role model or mentor.

Summary

- Holding onto grudges isn't healthy; resentment can poison your life.
- Releasing a grudge can be difficult for several reasons, but forgiving those who have hurt you lets you move on.
- Weighing the pros and cons of forgiveness can help you realize how much you have to gain by deciding to let go of past grievances.
- Forgiving yourself is just as important as forgiving other people.
- Learn how to say, "I'm sorry" to others, but never feel entitled to their forgiveness.
- You will feel calmer and happier when you learn how to develop compassion for yourself and others.

CHAPTER 8:

ANGER MANAGEMENT FOR PARENTS

Raising children is hard work. How ever much you love your son or daughter, they will get on your nerves sometimes. That's a normal part of parenting. No mother or father is perfectly calm at all times. On the other hand, for the sake of your family, you need to keep your anger in check around your children. Children who grow up with angry parents will copy those behaviors, and they are at increased risk of emotional and psychological problems.

In this chapter, we're going to look at why children and teenagers are challenging, and how to keep your cool when you feel your temper rising. Most of the time, your child isn't deliberately trying to aggravate you. They simply don't have the cognitive or linguistic skills to tell you how they feel. Your role as their parent is to work out the cause of their troublesome behavior and react accordingly.

Here are a few tips:

1. **Do not yell**
    Yelling might temporarily scare your child into submission, but it isn't a good long-term strategy. Shouting doesn't make your child understand why their behavior is inappropriate; it just shocks them into stopping. Parents who yell tend to have children who yell because their kids have learned that yelling lets you assert power over other people. Raising your voice only makes a difficult situation more tense.

    Instead, speak in a level tone and explain why your kid's behavior is out of line. You can then impose consequences, such as time out. Choose a mantra to repeat in your head when things start spiraling, such as "They aren't trying to hurt me," or "This will pass." If your children start yelling at one another, separate them until they both calm down.

2. **Take a bathroom break**

    If you feel as though your anger is spinning out of control, remove yourself from the room if you can. Tell your child that you're going to the bathroom and you'll be right back. Lock the door, take a few deep breaths, and remind yourself that everything will be OK.

3. **Ask yourself, "Is this behavior triggering something in me?"**

   Seeing your children inadvertently act out something upsetting from your own childhood can put you on edge.[47] For instance, if one of your children is bullying the other, this can trigger unpleasant memories of being teased by your own sibling. Staying self-aware keeps you from overreacting.

4. **Apologize to your child if you lose your temper**

   Apologizing won't make your child lose respect for you.[48] In fact, they will admire you for being mature enough to admit that you were in the wrong. It's a positive lesson to teach them. Tell them that being a loving family member means saying you're sorry when you hurt someone else. Tell them that you are working on controlling your temper and that everyone—even a grown-up—is a work in progress.

5. **Educate yourself**

   Children face different frustrations and challenges as they mature from babies to young adults, and you'll need to adapt your parenting strategies along the way. Prepare yourself by reading up on what you can expect. There are lots of reputable books available online. You can also ask your family doctor for recommendations.

6. **Do not label your child**

    Children are sensitive, and an offhand remark can stay with them for years. For example, if you call your child "lazy" because they haven't cleaned up their room for a while, they will quickly generalize from that remark and conclude, "Mom (or Dad) thinks I'm a lazy person."

    Focus on the behavior, not the child.[49] For example, it is better to say, "In this family, we do not bite each other" rather than "I can't believe you bit your brother—why do you have to be so awful all the time?" Labeling a child creates a self-fulfilling prophecy. If they've been labeled "the bad one," in time they will start living up to their reputation.

7. **Set reasonable rules, then follow through**

    Surprising as it may seem, children actually like rules and routines. The world is a big, scary, confusing place for a child, and rules give a sense of structure and security they can rely on. Rules keep children safe, and they also prepare them for school and the working world. When a child knows that breaking rules comes with consequences, they are more likely to think twice before making a bad decision. Self-control is a valuable skill that will benefit your child in every area of their life, and it will also help them grow into a well-balanced adult.

    Although you have the final say when it comes to house rules, you should ask your child for their input. Giving them a sense of ownership of rules means they will be more likely to stick to them. House rules should be realistic and age-appropriate. This might mean you have to set special rules for each child. Children have a keen interest in fairness, so explain precisely why everyone has a different set of rules and responsibilities. Remind them that when they get older, they will gain new rights and privileges.

8. **Help your child stick to the rules**

    Remove sources of unnecessary temptation. For example, if one of your house rules is that no one eats candy between meals, keep it out of sight.

Exercise: What Are Your House Rules?

Does your child know exactly what is expected of him or her? Draw up a list of "house rules" and keep it on display. If you already have a set of rules, do you need to update them?

9. **Don't focus on what your child shouldn't be doing—give them positive directions instead**

    For example, instead of saying "Don't pull the cat's ears," say "Stroke the cat's head gently." If your child hears an endless stream of "don't," "can't," and other negative words, they will start to assume they can never please you. In time, they might start wondering why they should even bother trying to behave properly. Be on the lookout for good behavior, and praise your child at every opportunity.[50]

10. **Be kind to yourself**
    You've already handled lots of tricky parenting situations, and you can do it again! All parents, no matter how confident they may seem, have moments where they feel their control of a situation slipping away. Everyone worries that they are doing a bad job, but most kids turn out OK. Show yourself some compassion.

11. **Slow down and listen**
    Children often act out when they feel their needs aren't being met. Their behavior may be a sign that they want more attention. Ask them, "What do you want right now?" or "Tell me how you feel." They might not be able to articulate precisely what's bothering them, but you might get a few clues.

12. **Remind yourself that disciplining your child is a kindness**
    If you don't discipline your child, they will grow into an adult with poor boundaries, a sense of entitlement, and difficulty in forming relationships.[51] Believe it or not, they may thank you someday for setting rules when they were growing up.

    Discipline and anger are not the same. Getting angry at a child is a form of punishment. Discipline is a form of guidance that shows your child how to make better choices. For instance, taking away your child's gaming console for a day because they hit their sister is a form of discipline. Losing your temper and screaming at them is a very basic and unsophisticated form of punishment.

13. Explain how you feel

Don't assume that your child knows why you are angry. Even if they do understand, it doesn't hurt to repeat the message. For example, if you are mad because they have drawn on the wall with a crayon, spell out exactly why their actions have triggered your anger. You could say, "I feel angry when you draw on the wall because it means the wall gets messy and I have to clean it." Very young children won't always understand you, but telling them about your feelings helps them learn that talking about emotions is normal and healthy.

When Your Teen Makes You Mad

Teenagers are notorious for driving their parents crazy, but you can maintain a positive relationship with your child as they go through adolescence. Try to see life from their perspective. Do you remember what it was like to be their age? Even if you loved your parents, you probably fought with them sometimes.

Teenagers are in a state of conflict. They want to separate themselves from the rest of the family and carve out their own identity. On the other hand, they don't yet have the emotional stability or knowledge to navigate the adult world, and they still need to look to their family for support. Adolescence is an exciting but scary time. Teens need independence, but they also need rules and boundaries.[52]

Here are a few tips if you're parenting a teen:

1. **Don't take their behavior personally**

    Almost all parents of teens have to tolerate a lot of frustration. It doesn't matter how great your parenting skills have been up to this point. Your child's brain is changing, and there's nothing you (or they!) can do about it. One day, your child will be an adult. The two of you might even be able to look back on this time and laugh about their antics.

    Teens are prone to mood swings. If they seem calm in the morning and grumpy in the afternoon, don't assume you've done anything wrong. Let them know you will always be there to talk and listen, then let them make the next move.

2. **Don't let your insecurities win**

    When your children are young, they idolized you. You were the center of their universe. It can be quite a shock when they grow up and start questioning your views and parenting skills. Try to keep your insecurities in check.[53] Children don't stop loving their parents when they become teenagers. In time, your relationship will improve. In the meantime, invest in your own self-development.

3. **Give your teen some credit**

    Their brains haven't yet matured, but teens can make sophisticated arguments and can be quite self-aware. In fact, they can show better judgments than many adults. You might not agree with their logic, but understanding their perspective at least gives you some common ground to work with. Don't belittle them. Although they may appear aloof and rebellious, teens often have low levels of self-esteem. They need firm but supportive parents who will show them respect.

When Your Relationship is Under Pressure

Having children puts the strongest of relationships under strain. Research shows that having a baby lowers marital satisfaction.[54] The effect is even greater if the pregnancy was unplanned. It's tempting to think that starting a family will bring you closer to your partner, but this is a myth; it will make your relationship worse if it was already on shaky ground. Having a child forces you to shift your identity within the relationship. You are no longer just a partner or spouse—you are also "Mom" or "Dad." It's common for new parents to go into "mom mode" or "dad mode."

This doesn't mean your relationship is doomed, but you do need to be mindful of the challenges to come. Although having children is linked to lower marital satisfaction, married couples with children are also less likely to get divorced.[55]

Sex and romance will have to take a backseat for a while after your child is born, but don't let emotional or physical intimacy fizzle out entirely. If you can afford it, hire a babysitter one night each week and go out as a couple. Try to talk about topics unrelated to children and parenting. Catch up on what's been happening at work, talk about your shared goals for the future, and try to relax in each other's company for a few hours.

If you're the primary caregiver, it's important that you take regular time for yourself. It isn't selfish to ask your partner to take over for a little while so you can get out of the house and do something you enjoy. The more relaxed and balanced you feel, the easier it will be to cope with the stresses of parenting. Spending time alone will make you a less angry parent.

Exercise: Taking Time for Yourself

Do you have any activities planned for yourself over the next week? If not, work with your partner to make sure you have at least a few hours alone, ideally outside your home. Just taking an afternoon to read a book in your local coffee shop can make a big difference in your mood.

No matter what relationship problems you are dealing with, it's important that you parent your children as a united front. Otherwise, your children will start feeling insecure. They will keep testing your boundaries, trying to establish what is and isn't acceptable behavior. If you are more lenient than your partner, you might become the "favorite parent," which will cause further resentment in your relationship.

SHOULD YOU ARGUE IN FRONT OF YOUR CHILDREN?

It isn't always bad to argue in front of your children. In fact, children who witness occasional mild to moderate parental conflict can benefit from it because it teaches them how to work through differences with another person. However, if your arguments are frequent, severe, or destructive, it's better if your children aren't around to see or hear them. Do not discuss sex or other "adult" issues around your children.[56]

Children, particularly young children, are not able to understand that they haven't made you angry. From their perspective, Mom and Dad are often mad, and it's probably their fault. If you can't agree on how to look after your children, you need to work with a therapist and learn how to stop your personal struggles affect your parenting style. Never use your child as a surrogate therapist. As an adult and responsible parent, it's your job to seek help from someone with enough emotional maturity to give it.

Summary

- It's normal to feel anger towards your children, whatever their age.
- You are your child's first role model, so it's your job to show them how to control anger and work with other people to solve disagreements.
- Consistent discipline and boundaries are essential for your child's development and wellbeing.
- As your child grows into a teenager, they will attempt to rebel against you while still needing your support.

- Children have less sophisticated reasoning and emotional regulation skills compared to adults. Most of the time, they are not trying to anger you.
- It is normal for marital satisfaction to drop when you have a child.
- Do not let your children witness destructive conflict.

CHAPTER 9:

ANGER & JEALOUSY

It's normal to occasionally feel jealous in your relationship. However, excessive jealousy gets in the way of real intimacy. Healthy relationships are built on mutual trust, not paranoia or fear. In this chapter, we're going to look at the causes of jealousy, why it is bad for your relationship, and how to fix it.

WHAT CAUSES ANGRY JEALOUSY?

Angry jealousy is a mix of anger and anxiety. It's triggered by a threat, which could be real or imagined. For example, if you feel jealous when your partner talks to their attractive colleague, you might feel as though their conversation could lead to the downfall of your relationship. Ultimately, this kind of jealousy is underpinned by a fear of loss.

Past experiences can also trigger jealousy. For example, if an ex-partner cheated on you, you might have formed the belief that "everyone cheats" or "no woman can be trusted." When these beliefs bleed over into your other relationships, you'll have problems.

A Little Jealousy is Normal

According to jealousy expert Robert Leahy,[57] jealousy can reflect your personal values, which isn't necessarily a bad thing. For example, if you are jealous in your marriage because you believe your spouse likes to flirt with other people, your jealousy stems in part from your belief in monogamous romantic relationships.

Psychologists also believe that the ability to feel jealous is actually an advantage. Historically, people who were vigilant around their partners could drive away their sexual rivals and pass on their genes.[58] However, this doesn't mean that feeling very jealous is normal, and it's not an excuse to treat your partner badly.

Why You Need to Address Angry Jealousy

Excessive angry jealousy triggers arguments. If you repeatedly ask your partner for reassurance, they will eventually start resisting. Unless they are a very compliant person, the two of you will start fighting about your need to control them.

In extreme cases, angry jealousy can be dangerous. People who try to protect their relationship or control their partner at all costs may resort to abusive, violent tactics to get what they want. If you have any tendency towards this kind of jealousy, it's absolutely essential that you learn how to handle it.

Jealousy drives people away. No self-respecting man or woman will stay in a relationship with someone who refuses to trust them. Try to see the situation from your partner's perspective. Would you be happy with someone who wanted you to account for your every move, who didn't trust you to behave appropriately with others, or resented your friends?

Exercise: What Does Your Jealousy Do for You?

Even destructive behaviors tend to serve a purpose. If you struggle with jealousy, remember that it probably comes from a desire to protect yourself. Write down three benefits of your jealousy. Does it stop you from feeling vulnerable? Does it keep your partner's attention focused on you at all times? Do you think your jealousy is a good way to "keep" hold of your partner, even if they dislike it?

PRODUCTIVE & UNPRODUCTIVE JEALOUSY

Productive jealousy triggers healthy, respectful conversations and behavior change. It is based in reality. Unproductive jealousy is based on gut feelings, hunches, or a need to gain a sense of power over a partner.

For example, suppose you feel jealous because your husband has been out with a group of male and female friends from work two nights this week, but you can't remember the last time he took you on a date. You feel jealous of the attention he's giving his female friends, and you've started to wonder whether he finds them more attractive and interesting than you. Your feelings are rational, so your jealousy is productive. Your next step would be to explain to your husband how you feel, using the communication techniques outlined in earlier chapters.

However, let's suppose your husband casually mentions over dinner that he grabbed coffee at lunchtime with a female co-worker. Your husband has only mentioned this woman a few times since she joined the company a year or so ago, and he regularly socializes with people of both sexes at his office. You feel a surge of anger and anxiety, even though there is no evidence that he has done anything inappropriate. This is an example of unproductive, irrational jealousy.

Exercise: Assess the Evidence

Take a step back from the situation by pretending that you are an impartial witness. What would you say to someone else in your position? Would any reasonable person conclude that you have a reason to feel uneasy, or is your jealousy based on nothing more than a hunch? If you aren't sure, ask a trusted friend or therapist whether you have reason to feel uneasy about your partner's behaviors.

HANDLING IRRATIONAL JEALOUSY

In a healthy relationship, both partners can talk about their feelings, even those we'd rather keep hidden. It's OK to admit you are jealous, as long as you acknowledge that it isn't your partner's fault, and it isn't up to them to fix it.

WHY REASSURANCE DOESN'T WORK

Jealous people tend to ask their partners questions like:

- "Do you still find me attractive?"
- "Why didn't you answer my call/text sooner?"

- "Is there anyone at work you think is attractive? Do you have a crush on them?"
- "Have you ever cheated on me? Do you ever want to?"
- "Do you still think about your ex? How often?"

Your partner's answers will probably make you feel better, but only for a while. Within a few days, your insecurity will come back. This kick starts a vicious cycle. You feel jealous, you ask for reassurance, your partner becomes annoyed, you worry that they no longer want to be with you, so you ask them for yet more reassurance. Rather than pester them for endless reassurance, you need to channel that energy into addressing your unhealthy thoughts.

Break free from the reassurance cycle by asking your partner to stop answering your questions. When you ask them to reassure you, they should say something like, "You asked me not to keep this cycle going, so I'm not going to answer you." At first, you won't like this new rule. You'll feel insecure and might even regret trying to work on your jealousy. But consider this: you'd probably feel insecure anyway because reassurance seeking doesn't bring you true peace of mind.

Within a few days, you'll realize that the only way to overcome your jealousy is to look inward and tackle the destructive thought patterns that are keeping you stuck.

Exercise: Jealousy Time

Set aside 10-20 minutes each day for jealous feelings. If you feel jealous at any other time, tell yourself that you can use your jealousy time to dwell on it later.

The "What If" Exercise

You coped with life before your relationship, and you could cope if it ended. Of course, you wouldn't want to split up with your partner, but it wouldn't be a catastrophe. You might truly believe that you'd never make it alone or that you'd die without them, but these beliefs are false.

Exercise: Imagining the End

Write a story in which your jealous thoughts turn out to be true, and your relationship comes to an end. Write down how you would feel in this situation. Write down what you would need to do next, such as serving divorce papers, selling your home, or arranging shared custody of your children. Finally, write how you would cope with your feelings and rebuild your life. Would you move to a new state? Retrain for a different career? Take up a new hobby? Visualize yourself living a successful life as a happy single person.

This is a challenging exercise, and it's best to do it alone in a quiet place. Once you push through your initial feelings of discomfort or even despair, you'll realize that you could survive if your partner left or cheated on you.

Retroactive Jealousy

If you feel jealous when you hear about things your partner did before your relationship—or even before the two of you met—you are suffering from retroactive jealousy. Retroactive jealousy is irrational because the third party doesn't pose any realistic threat to your relationship.[59]

Left unchecked, retroactive jealousy can spiral into an obsessive state. For example, if you are jealous of your partner's former spouse, you might be tempted to comb through their social media profiles or ask your partner a lot of questions about their relationship.

It's natural to be curious about your partner's past. However, although asking a few questions or even checking out their exes online is normal, subjecting your partner to a barrage of questions or obsessing over the past is not.

The best remedy for retroactive jealousy is to work on improving your self-confidence. When you appreciate your good qualities, you'll understand why your partner has chosen you instead of pining after someone from their past.

Of course, you may have been unlucky enough to start a relationship with someone who isn't over their ex-partner. If you know or suspect that you are just a stand-in or rebound partner, your jealousy might actually be somewhat rational. Take a step back and look at the evidence. Do you have any solid reason to believe that your partner is still fixated on their ex? For example, do they frequently mention them in conversation? Do they compare you to their former partner? If so, it's best to work with an individual or couples' therapist to resolve the underlying issues.

What are Your Core Beliefs?

Along with poor self-esteem, unhealthy core beliefs are a major cause of irrational jealousy. Core beliefs are strong and pervasive. If your core beliefs are positive, you'll interpret your partner's behavior in an optimistic light and trust them to do the right thing. If your core beliefs are based on unrealistic or negative views of relationships, you will be vulnerable to irrational jealousy.

Let's look at some negative core beliefs that keep irrational jealousy going.

1. **"I should feel secure all the time in my relationship."**

   No relationship is perfect. There will be times where one or both of you feel insecure. Fortunately, if you develop strong communication skills and take personal responsibility for your emotions, you can move past it. Feeling insecure doesn't mean you are weak or immature. It means you are human.

2. **"My partner should never find anyone else attractive."**

   People in monogamous relationships don't stop noticing other men and women. It's natural and normal to appreciate someone else's beauty. Of course, if your partner is brazenly staring at other people when you're together, you need to tell them you feel uncomfortable and set firm boundaries about how you behave around one another. But the occasional glance is no big deal. Think about all the people you've noticed on the street or at work over the years. You've probably forgotten most of them, and they didn't pose any threat to your relationship.

   This belief is also toxic because it can make you feel guilty for no good reason. If you sincerely believe that it's wrong to discreetly admire someone else, you'll end up feeling bad about yourself every time you look at an attractive stranger.

3. **"If two people find each other attractive, they are bound to get together."**
Let's say your partner meets someone they find attractive, and the other person returns their admiration. Does it mean they are destined to run off together and fall in love? Of course not—but jealous people tend to make this assumption, which is why they feel so threatened whenever their partner meets an attractive man or woman. Turn the question around. Ask yourself, "If I happened to meet someone I really liked tomorrow, would I necessarily run off with them?" In all likelihood, the answer is "No, because I love my partner."

4. **"If my partner flirts with someone, I must be ugly or not good enough for them."**
People flirt for various reasons, and it's rarely because their partner isn't good enough. Some people have naturally outgoing personalities and slip into "flirt mode" with little thought. Others like the attention; even though they are in a relationship, they flirt with others as a way of reassuring themselves that they are still attractive.

If your partner does tell you that you aren't good enough for them, that reflects badly on them, not you. A kind, emotionally mature person ends a relationship or at least tries to tackle their problems head-on instead of berating or insulting their partner. Do not waste your time trying to be "better" for someone who isn't deserving of you.

5. **"I have the right to know where my partner is at all times."**
Feeling insecure and wanting to keep tabs on your partner doesn't make you an abuser, but it can be a slippery slope. In short, you do not have the right to know your partner's whereabouts. You should not ask for your partner's passcodes, social media login details, or a minute-by-minute breakdown of their schedule.

There is one exception to this rule. If your partner has cheated on you and the trust has broken down in your relationship, it may be reasonable to ask them to check in with you more often. However, it's best to work with a couples' counselor if you need to negotiate these boundaries after infidelity. A professional will help you work out how to best restore trust in your relationship without suffocating your partner.

6. **"Someone cheated on me before. Therefore, I can't trust anyone."**
Holding back in a relationship can make you feel safe, but it makes true intimacy impossible. Forgiving the other person is key to shedding this belief. It simply isn't fair to generalize from a past

relationship and punish your partner for someone else's mistakes.

Exercise: When Did Your Jealousy Turn Out to Be Unfounded?

Write a list of occasions your jealous feelings turned out to be irrational. For example, perhaps you were convinced that your partner was out with someone else one evening when they said they were at home sick, but their friend or neighbor later confirmed they really were ill. Have you had similar experiences? Write them down. The point of this exercise is to show that gut feelings or hunches can be strong, but they aren't necessarily correct.

If your jealousy makes it impossible for you to concentrate on your work or studies, it's time to get help from a therapist. They can help you work out where your jealous tendencies stem from, and how to handle your irrational thoughts. If your partner has told you that your behaviors make them anxious or even scared, don't dismiss them. Take their feelings seriously and thank them for the wake-up call. It's hard to face up to our own faults, but you can learn to work through your jealous tendencies.

IS YOUR PARTNER JEALOUS?

Perhaps you aren't the jealous one in your relationship; maybe your partner feels insecure, and you are reading this chapter because you want to know how to handle it. The best approach is to validate their feelings without validating their need for reassurance. Tell them that you sometimes feel jealous too, and you understand what it's like, but you aren't going to waste your time giving them the same reassurances over and over again.

If you haven't done anything wrong, you should never accept responsibility for your partner's jealousy. It's their problem. You can support and encourage them, but you cannot force them to change. Remember too, that you are under no obligation to stay with them, even if they are trying hard to improve. If the relationship is making you unhappy, you have every right to decide that their jealousy is too much for you to deal with.

Nothing is Permanent

Finally, take a lesson from Eastern philosophy. Nothing is permanent, including your relationship. Although it's scary to realize that most things in life are beyond our control, accepting this fact is liberating. You can waste your time and effort trying to control your partner's behaviors and feelings. Alternatively, you can try to be your best self in your relationships and hope that the rest falls into place, all the while knowing that you'll be OK by yourself. It's up to you.

Summary

- Some jealousy is normal in a relationship.
- Jealousy is often mixed with anger, and it stems from a fear of loss.

- Jealousy can be rational or irrational, and you need to learn how to tell the two apart.
- Retroactive jealousy is especially hard to handle, even though those suffering from it know they are being irrational.
- If you hold unreasonable beliefs about relationships, you will be more vulnerable to jealousy.
- If your behavior makes your partner anxious or scared, it's time to get professional help.
- Letting go of your need to control a situation is key to overcoming jealousy and building a healthier relationship.

CHAPTER 10:

HANDLING ANGER AT WORK

Letting your anger get the better of you can cost you the job or career of your dreams. If you have an anger problem, it's essential that you learn a set of techniques for keeping your emotions under control at work. In this chapter, you'll discover how to keep cool when co-workers, customers, and your boss trigger your anger. If you're a team leader or manager, it's doubly important that you know how to stay professional under pressure. We'll look at a few techniques you can use to resolve common problems in teams.

If you're at home, or with your loved ones, you can take time out to process your feelings and calm down. But if you get mad in the middle of a meeting or have a fit of rage a few hours before a big deadline, you can't just walk away. Fortunately, you can learn how to manage your emotions, wherever you are.

What Makes You Mad at Work?

Exercise: Your Workplace Anger Triggers

Think back over the last three days you spent at work. What made you angry? Do you have a lot of different triggers, or do the same old issues tend to come up again and again?

Perhaps you already know what triggers your anger, and this is an easy exercise. But maybe you aren't sure why you feel so irritable. This list might help you pin down your triggers:

1. **Moving goalposts**
   Being asked to meet ever-shifting deadlines and objectives is enough to frustrate anyone. If you receive conflicting instructions that seem to change every ten minutes, it's normal to feel annoyed.

2. **Poor management**
   Poor management is one of the most common reasons employees quit their jobs.[60] Distant managers and micromanagers are both difficult to work with. It can be infuriating when your manager is distant and never seems to be around when you need them most. On the other hand, being micromanaged can leave you feeling patronized and suffocated.

3. **Violated expectations**
   When you sign an employment contract and start a new job, you have a set of expectations about what you will have to do, how you will be doing it, and

with whom you will be working. Unfortunately, it's not unusual for employees to be saddled with tasks that are way outside their job descriptions.

4. **Bias**

    If you are biased against a certain type of person, you may be quick to assume the worst of their behavior. For instance, if you tend to assume that women are prone to gossiping on the job, you might assume that your female colleagues must have been wasting time sitting around and talking if they haven't been able to meet a deadline.

    This works the other way around too—if you are forced to work with people who are bigoted or judgmental, it's hard to enjoy your work. You may feel on edge, always watching out for the next offensive comment.

5. **Unpleasant working conditions**

    Is your work environment too hot, too cold, too crowded, badly lit, or unsafe in some way? If your workspace is uncomfortable, you might be left feeling that your employers don't care about your well-being.

6. **Hostile co-workers**

    Spending every day in the company of rude, mean people is a test of anyone's patience. If you are being bullied, you might feel a difficult mix of emotions, including anxiety and sadness. According to a recent study, over 60 million US workers report being bullied at work.[61]

7. **Incompetent colleagues**
   If your colleagues aren't very good at their job, you might be left to pick up the slack. If you are forced to take on an informal leadership role to ensure the work gets done, you may feel annoyed and overburdened.

How to Stay Calm

In summary, it's normal to feel frustrated at work. What can you do to keep the peace? Here are some useful strategies to strengthen your working relationships:

1. **Use "we" to find common ground**
   When people get together at work to exchange ideas, some disagreement is inevitable.

   Use "we" language to imply you are willing to work with everyone else to find a solution, even if you think their ideas are nonsense.

   For example, let's say you are in a team meeting. Two team members argue in favor of a solution that you think is completely inappropriate. Instead of saying "I think you are wrong, and here's why," say "We all want this project to go as smoothly as possible, right? I'd like to point out a couple of reasons why this plan may not work."

2. **Use the "When, Feel, Need" model if you want someone to change their behavior**

   If a colleague is disrespecting you, use the "When, Feel, Need" model to tell them how you feel and what you would like them to do next time around.[62]

   For example:

   "*When* you put forward that idea for a new marketing campaign in this morning's meeting, I *felt* annoyed because I was the one who gave you that idea when we had coffee last Tuesday. I *need* you to acknowledge my contributions and to be given credit."

3. **Think twice before sending that email**

   A single email can be enough to get you fired. If you aren't sure whether you've struck the right tone, ask a trusted colleague to read it before you hit "Send." Another good tip is to wait at least an hour, preferably much longer, before sending it. If you can wait overnight and sleep on it, then so much the better.

4. **Stay politically savvy, but don't assume the worst**

   It's not just what you know and what you do at work that matters; it's also *who* you know. The relationships you have in the workplace can determine your career. Office politics are a fact of life, and it's smart to pay attention to social dynamics at work. Some people will undermine you just to get ahead, whereas others simply lack basic manners and respect for others. If you're unlucky, you might come across someone who appears charming on the surface, but then takes advantage of you when it suits them.

Cautious optimism is best. Assume that everyone is reasonable and professional until proven otherwise. Your colleagues are only human. Everyone makes mistakes or gets snappy sometimes. If you interpret every slight or argument against you as an act of malice, you'll be unhappy or angry most of the time.

5. **Leave work at work**

    Give yourself the chance to decompress every night after work.[63] Throwing yourself into a career can be psychologically and financially rewarding, but putting it before everything else in your life is a big mistake. If you suddenly lose your job, or half your team is replaced by people you don't especially like, your happiness will nosedive overnight. If you have a strong social network and a couple of enjoyable hobbies, these kinds of change won't hit you quite as hard.

    Create your own post-work ritual. You could listen to a specific podcast or artist, read a chapter of a book, do a few breathing exercises, or plan your evening. Try not to take your work home with you at night, and make it a rule to never work on the weekend or during vacation time. Overworking yourself raises your risk of stress, which in turn can lead to irritability, anger, and burnout.

How to Deal with Unfair Criticism

No matter how great we are, we all need feedback at work. Otherwise, how would we improve? Unfortunately, some people are terrible at giving constructive criticism. Being on the receiving end of unfair feedback can be maddening. How should you deal with it?

Try the following:

1. **Consider the source**

    Ask yourself this question: "Is this person really qualified to pass judgment on my work?" If the answer is "No," there's no need to take what they say personally. Perhaps they are new to the job, perhaps they are incompetent, perhaps they have an established reputation as a hostile leader, or maybe you have a good reason to believe they are trying to undermine you.

2. **Clarify what the other person meant to say**

    If you receive a strange or inappropriate piece of feedback, check that you've understood what the other person is trying to say. Sometimes, it can be hard to put criticism into words. Before you react, use your own words to tell them what you heard, and ask them if you've missed anything. Try to get the full story before jumping in to defend yourself. Open questions will encourage them to give you more detailed feedback.[64] For example, you could ask, "Why do you think that?" or "What do you think I can do about this?"

3. Remind yourself that your response could make a big difference

If you respond with anger or visible irritation, your reputation will take a hit. Try to see unfair criticism as an opportunity to deal with an anger trigger. Stay cool, and others will respect you as someone who can take feedback (whether or not the feedback was fair).

4. Look at the situation from another perspective

Assuming the person giving the criticism doesn't have a reputation for being generally hostile, consider whether there could be another reason for their behavior. Have there been lots of changes at work recently? Are they under a lot of pressure to meet a big deadline? There is no excuse for being unkind to other people, but putting yourself in their shoes can make it easier for you to deal with their behavior.

5. Try to find a piece of constructive feedback, no matter how small

If there is a grain of truth in what your critic says, acknowledge it. Agree that you have work to do, and tell them how you are going to address any gaps in your skills or knowledge. Most people, even when they are given management responsibilities, don't receive much training in giving feedback. A common mistake is to confuse behavior with character. For example, your boss might be frustrated because you have missed a couple of deadlines by a few hours each time.

In an ideal world, they would say, "You have missed your last two deadlines by four or five hours. This throws off my work for the week, and it means other people are inconvenienced. In the future, I need you to submit your work on time, or at least give me a day's notice if you are overloaded with work." If they have weak communication skills, they might say something like, "You're lazy and you never get anything done!" Try to look beyond generalizations and labels.

6. **Remind yourself of your recent successes**
   Receiving unfair criticism doesn't mean you are a failure, even if you find it hard to dismiss it. Pick yourself back up by thinking about what has gone right for you at work recently. Keep a list of achievements near your desk or on your phone and review them when you need a boost. Ask a trusted friend or colleague to remind you of your strengths.

7. **Ask for concrete suggestions on how you can improve**
   Once you have clarified precisely what your critic meant and the motivation behind their criticism,

ask what they would like you to do differently in the future. They might not be able to think of anything, in which case you can thank them politely for their feedback and move on. Otherwise, you can ask them to help you put together an improvement plan. Write it up and send a copy to them via email, or invite them to sign a printout. This holds them accountable if they later deny collaborating with you and prevents disputes in the future.

8. **After wrapping up the conversation, make a conscious decision to move on**

   Dwelling on the feedback will only drag you down. Move onto the next item on your to-do list. Resist the urge to analyze the conversation with your colleagues; you've got better things to talk about. The more quickly you can redirect your attention to something positive, the less power your critic will have over you.

Exercise: Making Sense of Feedback

The next time you get some feedback that seems unduly harsh, break it down into key points. Go through them one by one. If a bullet point is completely nonsensical, strike it out. If it contains a grain of truth, rewrite it as a more constructive sentence. For example, if your boss told you, "You're always late!" and you occasionally arrive five or ten minutes past your official start time, you could write, "You are sometimes late for work, and that needs to change."

Setting a Good Example

As an employee, you need to keep calm at work if you want to be taken seriously and keep your job. But if you're a leader, you have an additional responsibility—you need to set a good example for your team. Modeling a positive approach to conflict management sets the tone at your workplace, and fosters team success.[65]

Team members seldom agree on everything, and that's OK. Make it clear that everyone needs to respect the opinions of others, even if they completely disagree. Model the behaviors you'd like to see in your team. Invite everyone to share their ideas and give them time to talk. When you make a mistake and let your temper get the better of you, apologize. Never pretend to be a perfect leader—in any case, no such person exists. Your team will respect you for owning your mistakes.

When two or more members of your team disagree, it's your job to help them resolve the conflict. There are two main forms of conflict management: preventative measures and alternative dispute resolution. Preventative measures include communication skills training and setting out clear expectations regarding respectful behavior. Alternative dispute resolution might entail informal discussions or mediation.[66]

Some people have problems keeping their own anger in check yet have no trouble acting as peacemaker. But if you struggle to stay professional and unbiased when reconciling employees at work, it's a good idea to be proactive and ask your manager for training in conflict resolution.

Never ignore conflict in your team. The problem is unlikely to resolve itself. In fact, it will probably get worse. Minor issues can grow quickly if you don't address them. What's more, your team will resent you if you fail to step in and do your job.

Finally, try to create a positive atmosphere at work. When your team succeeds, make a point of praising them. When you have to deliver some constructive criticism, include some positive feedback if possible. If your team feels that their work is a safe place and their leader cares about their wellbeing, everyone is likely to be calmer, more productive, and less confrontational.

Handling Injustice at Work

Although we'd all like to believe that those who work hardest enjoy the greatest rewards, few workplaces are truly meritocratic. Lots of people get angry when they are passed over for a promotion they were promised, or when someone else gets all the credit for their ideas.

We are raised to believe that if we work hard, we'll get what we deserve. For a while, this belief serves us well. We are told that when we go to school, we'll get high grades if we study for our tests—and that's usually true. At college, we graduate if we put in enough work. Then, when we enter the adult world, it becomes apparent that these rules no longer apply. The most competent, kindest people do not always win. This is a painful realization.

The next time you feel frustrated by injustice at work, ask yourself this: Is there anything you can do to rectify the situation? If so, that's great news! Your next task is to figure out how, and then put your plan into action. If not, you need to let it go. In previous chapters, you learned how to move past grudges, work with difficult feelings, and grow your emotional intelligence. Unfair situations at work are the perfect opportunity to put these skills to good use. Practicing your anger management skills and coming to terms with unfairness builds your psychological resilience.

If you have grounds to report someone to your HR department or union, then do so, but don't get drawn into an ongoing battle with your co-workers or your boss. Keep your dignity intact and focus on doing the best job you can. Redirect your attention and think of the aspects of the job you do enjoy or appreciate. If a co-worker or boss has treated you unfairly, try to list a few times they treated you well.[67]

Use Your Employee Assistance Program

Some EAPs include psychotherapy and anger management training. Don't wait until a colleague—or worse, your manager—suggests that you should think about getting help to control your anger. Call your EAP hotline and talk about your options.

If you've noticed that the atmosphere at work is often tense, and people frequently get upset or angry, you could suggest tactfully that the company invest in communication skills training.

Is It Time to Move On?

Perhaps you've tried changing your outlook, improving your communication skills, or changing the way you handle grievances at work, yet still find yourself getting angry on a regular basis. It might be time to look for a new job, especially if you are relatively happy in other areas of your life.

Summary

- It's common to get angry at work.
- If you have to deal with unfair criticism, try to stay calm and understand the other person's perspective.
- Draw a firm line between work and home. Leave work at work.
- Consider using your EAP to access anger management training or counseling.
- If you are a leader, you need to be a good role model when it comes to emotional regulation.
- Despite your efforts, your current workplace might not be the best fit for you. Sometimes, it's better to look for a new job than attempt to fit in with those around you.

CHAPTER 11:

HOW TO HANDLE DIFFICULT PEOPLE

In this chapter, we're going to look at how you can keep your temper under control when dealing with difficult people. Whether it's your colleague, relative, neighbor, or even a so-called friend that is making your life hard, you need to be prepared. The good news is that, with practice, handling difficult people needn't be overly challenging. If you pay attention, you'll realize that many of them share the same behaviors and mannerisms.

DIFFICULT PEOPLE: THE MOST COMMON TYPES

It's impossible to fit everyone into neat little boxes, but difficult people generally fall into one of the following categories.

1. **Victims**

    Victims enjoy complaining. They seem to think the world is out to get them, and that everyone wants to see them suffer. Don't fall into the trap of trying to solve a victim's problems; they don't actually want to find solutions; they only want to moan about the unfairness of life. If you make constructive suggestions, you'll quickly become frustrated because they will shoot you down every time.

Victims aren't always easy to spot. At first, you may marvel at their misfortune. Judging by the stories they tell, you'd be forgiven for thinking they are the unluckiest person on the planet. In reality, although they might have had their fair share of bad luck, they take every opportunity to spin their stories into tales of woe.

The best approach when dealing with a Victim is to place the responsibility for solving their problems back where it belongs—on their shoulders. Ask, "What are you going to do about that?" or simply say, "That's too bad. I'm sure you'll figure it out, though." Do not get sucked into their negativity. Pretend that you have complete faith in their ability to turn their life around. Don't assume the role of their therapist or parent.

2. **Gossips**

Gossips take great delight in poking their noses into other peoples' affairs. They pass on sensitive information or rumors for their own entertainment. Some gossips know that their behavior is hurtful, whereas others are merely inconsiderate. If you discover that a gossip has been sharing your secrets with everyone else, you might soon find yourself getting very angry.

Be very careful whom you trust. Some people seem completely honest and reliable but will betray you later. You can't always spot these types; they are good actors. However, in most cases, you can tell who is most likely to pass on gossip. Watch someone's behavior. The way they talk about other people will tell you all you need to know. If someone has a reputation as a gossip, assume that the rumors are true.

When you start a new job or join a new club, keep your conversations light for the first few weeks. If you want to talk to someone about your personal problems, choose carefully. If they talk about other people behind their backs, it's only a matter of time before your problems become their conversation fodder.

3. **Know-it-alls**

These people believe they know everything about a given topic. Whatever the problem may be, they think they alone have all the answers. Some know-it-alls really are experts in their field, whereas others are just bluffing because they want to feel superior to everyone else. Because they assume they know best, they often ignore other people's contributions to a discussion.

If the know-it-all really is an expert in their domain, try to ignore their obnoxious behavior and focus on what you can learn from them. When you need to add your thoughts, interject firmly but politely. Say, "If you don't mind, may I add something here?" or "Excuse me for a moment, could I say something?" They won't like it, so be prepared for passive-aggressive behaviors such as eye rolling or loud sighs.

4. **Pessimists**

    Pessimists manage to find the downside in every situation. They effortlessly spot flaws and weaknesses and will happily talk about everything that could potentially go wrong, however unlikely. In some situations, it's actually good to have a pessimist around. For example, they are often highly detail-oriented and safety-minded. However, being in the same room as a pessimist for any significant length of time will drain your energy.

    When a pessimist starts making doom-laden predictions or talking about unlikely worst-case scenarios, ask them if they can think of a way to improve the situation. Wait patiently for their response. They will usually back off because they don't want to give a constructive alternative. Some pessimists just want to feel heard. Let them finish their point, nod, and thank them for their contribution before changing the topic of conversation. Like victims, pessimists thrive on negativity.

5. **Volcanos**[68]

    These people seem relatively calm most of the time but occasionally erupt in an angry outburst. Some volcanos have specific triggers that seem to set them off. Others are resentful people who swallow their anger for days, weeks, or even months, but gradually become overwhelmed by frustration. The first explosion you witness can be truly shocking because some volcanos have a carefully constructed façade of calm they use to hide their feelings. It's hard to trust a volcano because you know they are capable of exploding at any moment.

You'll need to set firm boundaries. Volcanos need to learn that they cannot get away with throwing temper tantrums. When you detect the first warning signs of anger, tell them that you won't have a conversation with them unless they treat you with respect. If they try to blow up at you, remove yourself from the situation and say you'll resume the conversation when they calm down.

6. **Narcissists**

Narcissists place their own needs and wants over everything else. They demand, and expect, special treatment and attention from everyone around them. They have little to no empathy and will manipulate people if doing so gets them whatever it is they want. A narcissist can be highly charming to people they see as special or powerful. If you are in a senior position at work, they might play the role of model employee when you're around, but abuse everyone else they deem "inferior."

Narcissists are attracted to vulnerability and drama. The best way to deter them is to appear polite, stable, and calm. Never reveal personal information to a narcissist, and don't spend any more time with them than absolutely necessary. Be prepared to enforce your boundaries. Narcissists tend to push people to see what they can get away with. Stand firm. Never cave to their demands for special treatment.

7. **Withdrawn individuals**

   These people choose to say very little, or even nothing at all. They are very difficult to work with because they don't volunteer any new ideas or opinions. Withdrawn people are, as a general rule, either extremely shy, introverted, or depressed.

   Don't put this kind of person on the spot; it's unlikely to help, and they will only resent you for making them uncomfortable. Ask them open-ended questions, rather than those that only invite "Yes" or "No" responses. If you suspect they have deeper problems, such as anxiety or depression, remember that it isn't your job to cure them. Show that you're willing to listen and that you respect their opinion, but don't expect them to suddenly morph into an extrovert.

8. **Bulldozers**

   These people are hard to miss. They don't bother consulting anyone before they act—they just charge ahead and assume that no one will question them. In conversations, they tell everyone what they think, and they will do so at length. Bulldozers don't necessarily think they are better or more knowledgeable than anyone else. Often, the problem is that they don't think of others at all.

Bulldozers require a blunt approach. To stop a bulldozer in full flow, raise a hand and say firmly, "Hold up a moment! There's something else we need to talk about here…" or "Hang on a second! You need to remember…" These people are not subtle, so you'll have to follow their lead. Tell them that you admire their enthusiasm and energy, but you'd like to hear from others too.

9. **People pleasers**

At first glance, a people pleaser may not seem difficult at all. They tend to be deferential and polite. The problem is that you never quite know what they are thinking, which makes it hard to build a genuine relationship.

Also known as "yes men," these people are so keen to be liked that they often over-promise and then under-deliver. People pleasers also have a habit of agreeing with the opinions of whoever they are talking to, which makes them appear flaky and untrustworthy. They are often insecure. Although they might have opinions and ideas of their own, they are reluctant to share them because they fear criticism.

If you aren't sure whether a people pleaser can follow through on a promise, ask them exactly how they plan to achieve their goal in the time available. If you want to know their opinion and the two of you are in a group situation, ask the people pleaser to share their thoughts first, so that they don't just go along with what other people are saying. Be sure to praise them when they make an original contribution to a discussion or project. This will encourage them to have more faith in their own abilities.

General Tips for Dealing with Difficult People

The first rule is to avoid taking their behavior personally. Difficult people have a set of communication methods and destructive attitudes that make them hard to work with. They have problems starting and maintaining relationships with almost everyone. If you get the chance to talk to other people who know them, you'll discover it's not just you that finds them challenging.

The second rule is to accept them as they are. Work on changing and improving yourself. Focus on adjusting your expectations of others, growing your EI, and controlling your temper. You don't have to waste your precious time and energy trying to teach a difficult person how to behave. If you want to give it a try, use positive reinforcement instead of punishment. If you have to work with a pessimist, be openly supportive when they voice a positive thought.

If you know a victim, act excited for them when they tell you about how they are going to solve one of their personal problems instead of complaining about how badly the world has treated them.

Try to see a difficult person as a gift. They give you the perfect opportunity to practice your anger management skills. Sure, you'd rather not have to deal with them, but every time you negotiate a challenging situation, your emotional intelligence and self-regulation will improve.

When Your Friend is a Difficult Person

Perhaps you've realized your friend fits into one of the above categories. What should you do? Start by reflecting on how you came to be friends with this individual. If you met in school or college, you might have bonded over your shared experiences and never moved on. These friendships can be a comforting link to the past.

You don't necessarily have to cut all difficult people out of your life, but you need to make informed choices. In general, it's best to see them only occasionally, stick to non-controversial topics, and keep your expectations realistic. Never keep someone in your life and hope that they will change. Some people do "wake up" and change their ways, but it isn't the norm.

Setting Boundaries

By taking a clear-eyed view of your friend's strengths and weaknesses, you can set appropriate boundaries. Boundaries let you enjoy your friend's positive traits while protecting you from their toxic behaviors.

For instance, you may appreciate your narcissistic friend's charm and energy, which makes them a great companion when you want to go out to a bar or club on a Friday night. However, they probably have an inability to offer you meaningful emotional support because they are so engrossed in their own drama—and they always seem to have a lot of drama going on.

In this example, you could set the following boundaries:

- "When I talk to this person, I will keep the conversation light and avoid talking about my deepest, most personal problems."
- "I will see this person no more than once a month, and always in a busy social setting."
- "If my friend tries to involve me in their current drama or crisis, I will politely shut down the conversation."

Difficult people can keep their place in your life, but they need to be managed with care. Setting boundaries isn't just key for managing difficult friends. You also need to practice adjusting your expectations and boundaries when dealing with difficult relatives, colleagues, and any other toxic people you see on a regular basis.

Summary

- Anyone can make us angry, but there are some types of people who are especially difficult.
- Learning about the most common types of difficult people, and how to handle them, will help you keep your temper under challenging conditions.
- Difficult people come in several varieties. They include victims, bulldozers, know-it-alls, and volcanos.
- Try to reframe frustrating experiences with difficult people as valuable opportunities to practice your anger management skills.
- If you have a friend who happens to be a difficult person, you may need to limit your contact, readjust your expectations, or both.

CHAPTER 12:

LIFESTYLE CHANGES & ANGER MANAGEMENT

You can use the anger management techniques in this book to cope with your anger on a moment-by-moment basis, but leading a healthier lifestyle will make it easier to keep your temper under control over the coming days, weeks, months, and beyond. In this chapter, you'll learn how and why your alcohol intake, diet, daily routine, self-talk, and goal-setting habits can empower you to live a calmer life.

Alcohol & Anger

We briefly looked at the relationship between alcohol and anger earlier in this book. Let's examine this issue in more detail.

Any substance that alters your mood or state of mind can make it harder to control your anger. If you drink alcohol on a regular basis, ask yourself why. It's normal to have a few drinks occasionally at a social gathering, or to reward yourself with a glass of wine at dinner after a long week.

However, if you often drink to change your feelings or to deal with stress, it's smart to re-examine your relationship with alcohol.

After your first drink or two, you probably feel relaxed. This is because alcohol is a depressant, meaning it slows down areas of the brain responsible for behavioral and emotional inhibition. However, as you consume more alcohol, it starts to affect other parts of your brain, and you might no longer feel so good. Some people become more anxious, upset, or angry than usual.[69]

If you regularly drink too much alcohol, you are at greater risk of developing depression and other mood disorders. This is because excessive alcohol consumption disrupts the delicate balance of neurotransmitters in the brain. The Center for Disease Control and Prevention recommends that women have no more than one alcoholic drink per day and that men should limit themselves to two.[70] Aim for a few alcohol-free days each week, as this lowers your risk of developing an addiction.

According to UK charity Drinkaware, alcohol can make some people more likely to become aggressive. Alcohol changes the way you perceive the world, and it encourages your brain to focus on any potential threats. It can make you develop tunnel vision, and even minor inconveniences can soon become triggers. For example, if you have been drinking, you are more likely to react more quickly and inappropriately than usual if you think your partner is flirting with someone else at the bar.[71]

However, alcohol cannot transform someone's personality. If you are usually calm and reasonable, it's unlikely you will be prone to anger when you have a few drinks. On the other hand, if you have a tendency towards becoming angry—which psychologists call "trait anger"—alcohol will make it worse. It's your responsibility to understand how alcohol affects you and to make sensible choices. You don't have to give it up entirely, but sticking to safe limits will improve both your relationships and your health. Drug and alcohol abuse isn't an excuse to treat anyone else badly.

Exercise: Keeping an Alcohol Log

If you drink alcohol regularly, track your consumption for a week. Count the number of units you consume. (You can normally find this information on the packaging or label, or you can research the typical number of units online.) Do you need to cut back? Do you notice that your mood gets worse when you've been drinking?

ILLEGAL DRUGS & ANGER

Stimulant drugs, such as cocaine and amphetamines, make people more prone to anger and aggression. They can trigger delusions and paranoia, which in turn can drive violent behavior. Hallucinogenic drugs, such as LSD and PCP, can also cause aggression if a user experiences a "bad trip" that frightens them. PCP increases pain tolerance, meaning users feel able to keep attacking other people (or themselves) even when they are badly injured.

Marijuana is a sedating drug, not a stimulant, and it doesn't trigger anger or aggression for most users.[72] However, some people feel more paranoid or anxious than usual after taking it, which can result in angry outbursts. Research also suggests that if you have an existing anger problem, you are more likely to feel irritable and aggressive when withdrawing from regular marijuana use.

If you misuse drugs or alcohol, managing your anger will be much easier if you get help. If you have a good relationship with your doctor, start by discussing the problem with them. They can recommend a suitable therapist or rehab facility.

In the US, UK, and several other Western countries, every major city has 12-step groups for people struggling with dependency and addiction issues. The 12-step model doesn't work for everyone, but Alcoholics Anonymous (AA) and Narcotics Anonymous (NA) meetings are a great place to find support from people in similar circumstances. There are lots of free helplines and email-based services you can call or message for advice. Use Google to search for resources in your country or local area.

Caffeine & Anger

Ninety percent of the global population uses caffeine in some form, and 80% of American adults consume it on a daily basis.[73] It's common knowledge that caffeine can make you feel more alert. Many of us enjoy a cup of coffee or tea in the morning to jump-start the day.

In moderation, caffeine doesn't usually cause serious side effects. However, research suggests that consuming too much can trigger hostility and anxiety. These effects are so significant that some psychiatrists have recommended that patients in psychiatric wards be encouraged to try decaffeinated beverages instead of their regular caffeinated drinks.[74]

As a rule, sticking to 200-300 milligrams per day—which is equivalent to approximately four cups of coffee—should protect you from these problems.[75] However, some of us are unusually sensitive to caffeine. If you drink a lot of tea or coffee, try cutting back on the amount you drink per day. You could also experiment with decaffeinated options. Caffeine withdrawal can cause unpleasant symptoms, such as headaches and irritability, so cut back gradually.

How Much Stress Can You Handle?

A lazy life of doing nothing would drive most people crazy. On the other hand, working 12-hour days isn't healthy either. We all have our own optimal stress levels. Keeping busy helps you develop a more balanced perspective on life and stops you from ruminating on negative thoughts, but trying to cram too much into your schedule leaves you vulnerable to stress, resentment, and anger.

If you have too much work to do, or your calendar is full of commitments and obligations, you may need to practice saying "No." For example, if your boss asks you to take on extra work, it's best to be honest rather than saying

"Yes" and risking burnout. Another common pitfall is accepting too many invitations to social events. Even if you are an extrovert who loves going out and seeing family and friends, it's important to set limits.

Take regular vacations and day trips if possible. You may not be able to afford to go away to an exotic location, but you can probably arrange an afternoon at a local tourist attraction or a picnic in the park. Don't feel guilty about taking time away from work or your studies. We all need to unwind sometimes.

PICK GOALS THAT WORK FOR YOU

What are you working towards in your life right now? Living someone else's life, or striving for goals someone else has chosen on your behalf, is enough to make anyone feel resentful. You'll be calmer and more satisfied in the long run when you make plans that align with your ambitions and personal values.

Exercise: What Are Your Goals?

Do you have short-, medium-, and long-term goals? Effective goals are specific, measurable, achievable, relevant, and time-bound. For a well-rounded life, you need to set goals for your work, relationships, and personal development. Do you know how you are going to achieve each goal? Do you need to break them down into subgoals?

If you aren't sure where you are going, who could help you make some plans? Do you need to speak to a therapist, a career counselor, or a personal development coach? When you are working toward a goal, you'll find it easier to keep minor annoyances or setbacks in perspective. You can remind yourself that you have a broader plan or vision, and most people or situations just aren't that important in the long run.

Food & Your Mood

What you eat, and when you eat it, can make a big difference in how you feel. According to dietitian Frances Largeman-Roth, keeping your blood sugar stable by eating moderate amounts of healthy food throughout the day will keep your temper on an even keel.[76] Getting too hungry will make you prone to irritability. Choose snacks that boost your serotonin levels, such as popcorn or salted peanuts. Aim for a balanced diet high in fruits, vegetables, lean proteins, and complex carbohydrates.

When it comes to fats, it's important to pay attention to the type you eat. According to a study by researchers at the University of California, eating too many trans fats may make you more aggressive.[77] Trans fats are most commonly found in processed and fried foods, such as pizzas, donuts, cakes, and margarine. Some meat and dairy products, such as beef, contain trans fats in small quantities. Not only do trans fats have a negative effect on your mood, but they also raise your risk of heart disease.

For the sake of your physical and mental health, try to eat a moderate amount of healthy fats, such as those found in olive oil, avocados, nuts, seeds, and oily fish. As a general guideline, healthy fats are those that stay in a liquid state at room temperature.[78]

ARE YOU ON A DIET? WHY WEIGHT LOSS MAKES YOU GRUMPY

If you're on a diet, you may feel more easily annoyed than usual. When you are trying to count calories, grams of fat, or any other macronutrient, you have to put more thought than usual into what you are going to eat, how much, and when.

Making these choices on a daily, or even hourly, basis takes a lot of self-control and discipline. Willpower is a finite resource. If you are channeling all your willpower into monitoring your diet, you'll have less mental energy left for controlling angry or aggressive urges.[79]

You can prevent diet-induced crankiness by automating your dietary decisions. For example, if you prep your meals a week in advance, you won't have to spend precious mental energy figuring out what to eat every evening. Allow yourself regular, planned treats. Depriving yourself of all your favorite foods will eventually cause you to binge, which will make you even more frustrated.

MOVE MORE

Many formal anger management programs encourage participants to take up regular exercise. Maybe you aren't a natural athlete, but that doesn't mean you can't benefit from working out. Even couch potatoes feel better when they start moving around. You don't need to exercise for hours at a time either. The current recommendation for American adults is a minimum of 150 minutes of moderate-intensity exercise each week. More is better. Include strength and flexibility training along with cardio.

Take Sleep Seriously

Everything feels easier after a decent night's rest. If you aren't sleeping well, you are more likely to feel irritable and short-tempered. Not everyone needs eight hours' sleep every night, so adjust your schedule until you feel better. If you share a bed with a partner, you don't have to turn in for the night just because they are ready to sleep.

Some people can get to sleep quickly, but then wake up in the night and find it hard to doze off again. If you have this problem, don't lie awake in bed for more than 20 minutes. Get up and do something calming until you feel tired again, such as a jigsaw puzzle. Learn to tell the difference between feeling tired and feeling sleepy. Tiredness is a feeling of being "worn out" or fatigued, whereas sleepiness is the feeling that you could drop off at any moment. Try to wait until you are sleepy before going to bed.

To avoid over stimulating your nervous system, do not work out or drink caffeinated beverages in the late afternoon or evening. Keep your room dark; invest in blackout blinds or curtains if necessary. Never use your phone, laptop, or other electronic device in bed, and don't watch TV. Your bedroom should be reserved for sleep, physical intimacy, and light bedtime reading if you want to wind down for a few minutes before turning off the light.

Keep Learning

As you discovered in Chapter 5, anger is often tied up with shame, sadness, and fear. It can also go hand-in-hand with boredom.[80] If you feel trapped and frustrated by your everyday routine, or feel like your personal or professional growth has been stunted, do something to address it.

Making a few minor changes, like taking up a new hobby or tweaking your daily routine to allow for more enjoyable activities, might be all you need. If you've been spinning your wheels for months or even years, it's time for a radical life overhaul. Perhaps your job isn't intellectually challenging anymore, and you need to find a new one. Or maybe you've outgrown your partner, and it's time to either work together to improve your relationship or cut ties.

How Do You Talk to Yourself? Why Positive Self-Talk is so Important

Wouldn't it be wonderful to have a loving, supportive person beside you all day, encouraging you to keep on going, even when everything feels too much to handle? When you fix your self-talk, you'll become your own cheerleader.

When you feel your temper flaring up, try telling yourself the following:

- "I can control my anger."
- "I can and will calm down."

- "I'm doing the best I can."
- "It's OK to feel sad or hurt."
- "The only person who can make me angry is me."
- "How would my role model handle this?"

When you succeed at work or achieve something significant in your personal life, give yourself a pat on the back. Tell yourself, "I did really well!" or "I'm a capable, talented person." When practiced on a daily basis, positive self-talk will improve your confidence. You will come to see yourself as a calmer, happier individual. Inappropriate anger and aggressive behavior will no longer feel quite so natural. As a bonus, you'll gradually become more optimistic.[81] If you focus on the positives in your life, the world will seem brighter.

Choose a couple of your favorite positive phrases and place them where you'll be able to see them every day. For example, you could set them as a screensaver or wallpaper on your phone, or write them on sticky notes and place them on your computer monitor.

If you fall back into your old ways, self-talk can help you move on and learn from the experience. For example, instead of telling yourself, "I'll never improve, I'm always going to be angry!" you could tell yourself something like, "I got mad, but I can forgive myself, learn from this, and move on."

Summary

- To stand the best chance of handling your anger, you need to use both short-term and long-term strategies.
- Limiting alcohol use, moderating your caffeine intake, and abstaining from illegal drugs are important for good anger management. Seek professional help if appropriate for your situation.
- Find your optimal stress level, and structure your activities and time accordingly.
- Eating a suitable diet, getting enough exercise, and practicing proper sleep hygiene will help you feel emotionally balanced.
- When you choose goals and a lifestyle that align with your personal values, you will find life more meaningful and less frustrating.
- Chronic boredom can be an anger trigger. Take a careful look at your day-to-day routine and look for opportunities to make your life more interesting.
- Choosing to use positive self-talk will help you stay optimistic and build a healthier self-image.

CONCLUSION

Congratulations on working your way through this book! You should be feeling calmer, more empowered, and ready to tackle life's challenges without resorting to fits of rage, temper tantrums, or passive aggression. Take a moment to feel proud of yourself. Changing your behaviors, thought patterns, and attitudes is tough. It takes a lot of courage and inner strength to face and fix your weaknesses.

If you have children, your relationship with them will be stronger than ever. If you are married or in a long-term relationship, your partner will feel able to open up to you in new ways. Your colleagues at work will also notice a change for the better. They might not be able to put their finger on it at first, especially if you used to show your anger in subtle ways, but they'll certainly feel happier around you.

When you make significant changes in your life, it's normal to have a few lapses. You may occasionally backslide, especially in the first few weeks. Don't give up. Forgive yourself, reread the chapters that speak to you most, and just keep doing your best. No one is perfect. Remember, it's healthy to feel angry in some situations.

By taking responsibility for your own anger, you will inspire others to change. If you're a parent or work with young people, your self-development will benefit the next generation. We all need to play our part to make the world a happier, safer place, and your personal self-development is the perfect place to begin.

THANKS FOR READING!

I really hope you enjoyed this book, and most of all got more value from it than you had to give.

It would mean a lot to me if you left an Amazon review—I will reply to all questions asked!

Simply find this book on Amazon, scroll to the reviews section, and click "Write a customer review".

Or alternatively, please visit www.pristinepublish.com/angermanagementreview to leave a review.

Be sure to check out my email list, where I am constantly adding tons of value. The best way to get on the list currently is by visiting www.pristinepublish.com/empathbonus and entering your email.

Here I'll provide actionable information that aims to improve your enjoyment of life. I'll update you on my latest books, and I'll even send free e-books that I think you'll find useful.

Kindest regards,

Judy Dyer

Also by
Judy Dyer

Grasp a better understanding of your gift and how you can embrace every part of it so that your life is enriched day by day.

Visit: www.pristinepublish.com/judy

REFERENCES

[1] Okuda, M., Picazo, J., Olfson, M., Hasin, D.S., Liu, S., Bernardi, S., & Blanco, C. (2016). Prevalence and Correlates of Anger in the Community: Results from a National Survey. CNS Spectrums.

[2] Akers, M., & Porter, G. (2018). *What is Emotional Intelligence?*

[3] Sissons, C. (2018). *What happens when you get an adrenaline rush?*

[4] NHS UK. (2016). *Why am I so angry?*

[5] Morin, A. (2015). *7 Myths About Anger (and Why They're Wrong).*

[6] Ibid.

[7] Mind. (2013). *How to cope with anger.*

[8] Ibid.

[9] Legg, T.J. (2019). *Do I Have Anger Issues? How to Identify and Treat an Angry Outlook.*

[10] American Academy of Neurology. (2004). *Anger, Negative Emotions May Trigger Stroke.*

[11] Williams, J.E., Paton, C.C., Sieglar, I.C., Eigenbrodt, M.L., Nieto, F.J., & Tyroler, H.A. (2000). Anger Proneness Predicts Coronary Heart Disease Risk. *Circulation.*

[12] Veroude, K., Zhang-James, Y., Fernandez-Castillo, N., Bakker, M.J., Cormand, B., & Faraone, S.V. (2015). *Genetics of Aggressive Behavior: An Overview. American Journal of Medical Genetics.*

[13] Dvir, Y., Ford, J.D., Hill, M., & Frazier, J.A. (2014). Childhood Maltreatment, Emotional Dysregulation, and Psychiatric Comorbidities. *Harvard Review of Psychiatry.*

[14] Sheffield Morris, A., Silk, J.S., Steinberg, L., Myers, S.S., & Robinson, L.R. (2007). The Role of the Family Context in the Development of Emotion Regulation. *Social Development.*

[15] Scott, E. (2019). *How to Manage Anger and Stress.*

[16] Office on Women's Health. (2018). *Premenstrual dysphoric disorder (PMDD).*

[17] Shimer Bowers, E. (2013). *Low Testosterone Can Make Men Grumpy.*

[18] Felman, A. (2019). *How does diabetes affect mood and relationships?*

[19] Butler, C., & Zeman, A.Z.J. (2005). Neurological syndromes which can be mistaken for psychiatric conditions. *Journal of Neurology, Neurosurgery & Psychiatry.*

[20] Martin, S. (2017). *How to Challenge Cognitive Distortions.*

[21] Morin, A. (2019). *11 Anger Management Strategies That Can Help You Calm Down Fast.*

[22] Denworth, L. (2017). *The Inside Story of How Slow Breathing Calms You Down.*

[23] Anxiety and Depression Association of America. (n.d.). *Exercise for Stress and Anxiety.*

[24] National Sleep Foundation. (n.d.). *Can Music Help You Calm Down and Sleep Better?*

[25] Liu, J., Lemay Jr., E.P., & Neal, A.M. (2018). Mutual cyclical anger in romantic relationships: Moderation by agreeableness and commitment. *Journal of Research in Personality.*

[26] Poulson, A. (n.d.). *How to express anger effectively: Nonviolent communication.*

[27] Lisita, E. (2013). *The Four Horsemen: Criticism, Contempt, Defensiveness, and Stonewalling.*.

[28] Martin, R. (2015). *5 Ways to Deal with Angry People.*

[29] Brandt, A. (2016). *Is Your Anger a Cover for Shame?*

[30] Ibid.

[31] Mayer, J.D. (2004). *What Is Emotional Intelligence?* UNH Personality Lab.

[32] Jack, R.E., Garrod, O.G.B., Yu, H., Caldara, R., & Schyns, P.G. (2012). Facial expressions of emotions are not culturally universal.

[33] Webb, J. (2019). *Do These 5 Things to Increase Your Emotional Intelligence.*

[34] Andrews, M. (n.d.). *How to Improve Your Emotional Intelligence.*

[35] Eurich, T. (2018). *What Self-Awareness Really Is (and How to Cultivate It).*

[36] Ibid.

[37] Bradt, S. (2010). *Wandering mind not a happy mind.*

[38] Eisler, M. (n.d.). *What's the Difference Between Meditation and Mindfulness?*

[39] Smookler, E. (2019). *Beginner's Body Scan Meditation.*

[40] Tartakovsky, M. (2018). *A Mindful Practice to Fully Feel Your Anger.*

[41] EOC Institute. (n.d.). *Harnessing Neuroplasticity: 9 Key Brain Regions Upgraded Through Meditation.*

[42] O'Brien, M. (n.d.). *R.A.I.N: A Four-Step Process For Using Mindfulness In Difficult Times.*

[43] Khoddam, R. (2014). *The Psychology of Forgiveness.*

[44] Plante, T.G. (2014). *7 Rules of Forgiveness.*

[45] Lindberg, S. (2018). *How to Forgive Yourself.*

[46] Ackerman, C. (2017). *9 Self-Compassion Exercises & Worksheets for Increasing Compassion.*

[47] Wallace, M. (2017). *Managing Parental Anger.*

[48] Ibid.

[49] Steward, M. (2013). *6 Tips to Avoid Labeling Your Child.*

[50] Channel 4. (2013). *Supernanny: Parenting Advice.*

[51] WebMD. (n.d.). *Parents, Kids, and Discipline.*

[52] Teen Therapy Center of Silicon Valley. (2014). *10 Ways To Set Appropriate Boundaries With Teens.*

[53] Berry, M. (n.d.). *File This Under: Things To Read When Your Teen Is Driving You Insane.*

[54] Johnson, M.D. (2016). *Decades of Studies Show What Happens to Marriages After Having Kids.*

[55] Ibid.

[56] Divecha, D. (2014). *What Happens to Children When Parents Fight.*

[57] Leahy, R.L. (2008). *Jealousy Is a Killer: How to Break Free from Your Jealousy.*

[58] Ibid.

[59] Billings, J. (2018). *Retroactive Jealousy vs 'Regular' Jealousy in a Relationship.*

[60] Heathfield, S.M. (2019). *Top 10 Reasons Why Employees Quit Their Jobs.*

[61] Workplace Bullying Institute. (2017). *2017 WBI US Workplace Bullying Survey.*

[62] Premack, R. (2018). *If you're angry at work, you shouldn't pretend everything is okay—do these 6 simple things instead.*

[63] Boon, E. (n.d.). *Managing Your Emotions at Work.*

[64] Conley, R. (2015). *Surviving Friendly Fire: 8 Tips for Dealing with Unfair Criticism.*

[65] Burton, L. (2017). *Managing Conflict in the Workplace: A Guide for Line Managers.*

[66] Ibid.

[67] Mayer, D. (2016). *4 Ways To Bounce Back When You're Treated Unfairly At Work.*

[68] Buckley, C. (n.d.) *10 examples of difficult people.*

[69] Verywell Mind. (2019). *The Link Between Alcohol and Aggression.*

[70] Centers for Disease Control and Prevention. (2016). *Fact Sheets – Moderate Drinking.*

[71] Drinkaware. (2019). *Alcohol and aggression.*

[72] Alcohol & Drug Abuse Institute. (2013). *Marijuana and Aggression.*

[73] Venosa, A. (2015). *Caffeine In Coffee Could Be Messing With Your Mood: Studies Link Caffeine To Anxiety, Depression.*

[74] Winston, A.P., Hardwick, E., & Jaberi, N. (2018). *Neuropsychiatric effects of caffeine. BJPsych Advances.*

[75] McCoy, W. (2018). *Can Caffeine Make You Angry?*

[76] Largeman-Roth, F. (n.d.). *Your Anger Management Menu.*

[77] Golomb, B.A, Evans, M.A., White, H.L., & Dimsdale, J.E. (2012). Trans fat consumption and aggression.

[78] Leonard, J. (2018). *What are the most healthful high-fat foods?*

[79] Melnick, M. (2011). *The Cranky Dieter Explained: How Self-Control Makes You Angry.*

[80] Markman, A. (2012). *What Is Boredom?*

[81] Jantz, G.L. (2016). *The Power of Positive Self-Talk.*

Printed in Great Britain
by Amazon